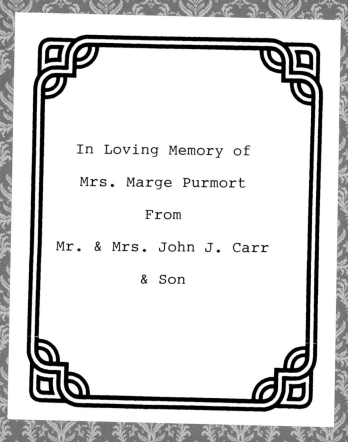

W9-BGW-454

FLOWER ARRANGING

The complete guide for beginners

JUDITH BLACKLOCK

The Flower Press

Published by
The Flower Press Ltd
3 East Avenue
Bournemouth
BH3 7BW

A CIP catalogue record for this book is available from the
British Library.

ISBN-13: 978-0-9552391-7-5

Design: Amanda Hawkes

Printed and bound in China by C & C Offset Printing Co., Ltd.

CONTENTS

INTRODUCTION

Contrary to many preconceptions you really do not have to be artistic or to study for years to be able to arrange flowers. If you follow the straightforward, logical instructions in this book you will soon be able to create designs that will give delight.

I have written this book so that anyone can arrange flowers successfully. It is not rocket science but there are a few things you need to absorb and digest, such as:

- what flowers and foliage are available – similar to a cook's knowledge of herbs and spices
- the 'mechanics' – a word that describes the means of making stems behave and keeping them in place
- how to combine your flowers and foliage to best effect
- the elements and principles of design (which are not as complicated as they sound)
- the best way to care for your plant material, so that it lasts for as long as possible.

Having taught for many years I know that confidence is gained by learning in a step-by-step fashion, whatever a student's background or previous experience. Consequently, most of the designs in this book have been broken down into simple stages that are easy to follow. This formula will enable you to learn without pain and to develop your new skills quickly. I do not believe in teaching a particular style. I believe that if you have a strong grounding you can build up your confidence and develop your own personal and original style with ease.

As your enthusiasm gains momentum, you will notice flower displays all around you and you will want to know how they were created. This book will also help you to explore these more challenging designs and encourage you to take the ideas and improve and adapt them to your personal taste, using the foliage and flowers available to you, whether grown or purchased. I have written longer, more comprehensive books for those who wish to take their learning further but I believe that this beginners' book will enable aspiring flower arrangers to have success every time.

If this book has whetted your appetite for learning, there are lots of avenues to explore. Why not join one of the UK's thousands of Flower Clubs that are affiliated to NAFAS (The National Association of Flower Arrangement Societies, www.nafas.org.uk).
You could have lessons at my flower school in Knightsbridge, London SW1 (www.judithblacklock.com) and you could subscribe to a magazine such as *The Flower Arranger*, which I edit. Gaze in shop windows, read books, visit hotels and churches to assess the flowers and you will never stop learning or enjoying the best hobby in the world.

Happy flower arranging.

Judith Blacklock

$\mathcal{B}$uying top-quality flowers is vital if you want them to last. The first part of this chapter describes how to check to ensure that you are buying the freshest available. You will also need foliage or greenery to accompany your flowers and you will find illustrations of leaves or shrubs that are often used in flower designs. Many of these are mentioned in the following chapters.

Having purchased the freshest flowers, you need to condition them so that they will last for the maximum amount of time. The treatment is quick and simple but it does work. Details are given in this chapter, along with myths that work and those that do not.

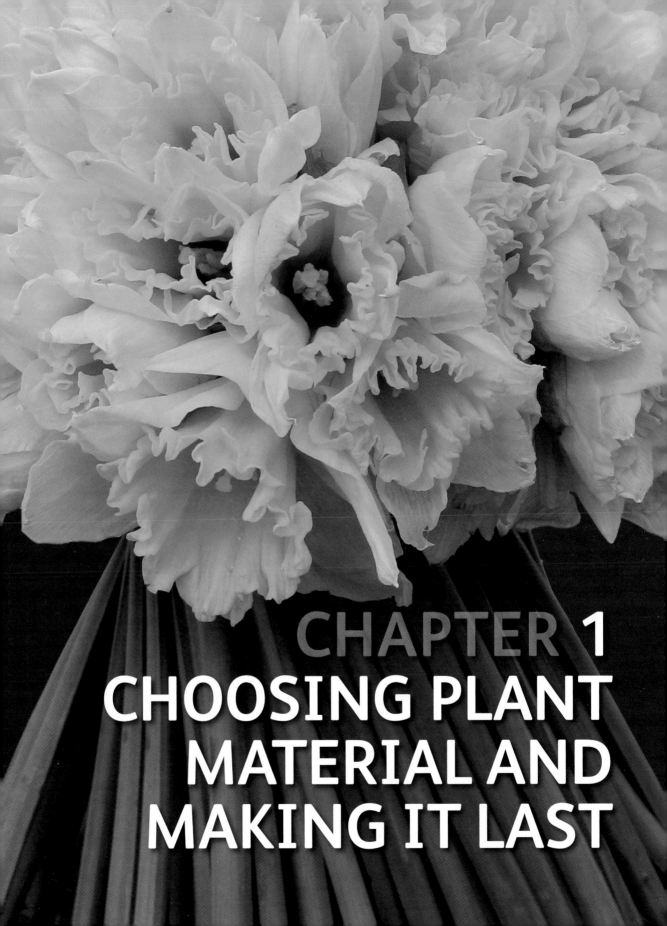

CHAPTER 1
CHOOSING PLANT MATERIAL AND MAKING IT LAST

A–Z OF HOW TO PURCHASE 100 QUALITY FLOWERS

Choosing your flowers is a very satisfying part of the creative process. Many factors can influence your choice of bloom:

- colour, shape and size
- fragrance
- available budget
- who the arrangement is for
- where the arrangement will be placed

Where to buy flowers

Depending on your requirements, flowers can be purchased from the following outlets:

Supermarkets

Advantages
- inexpensive flowers
- easy to purchase
- flowers can be returned if sub standard

Disadvantages
- according to the individual store the flowers may have been well looked after or ignored
- limited range of flowers
- foliage extremely limited

Street flower stalls

Advantages
- inexpensive flowers
- easy to purchase

Disadvantages
- often open to the elements, which can limit their life
- wrapping options limited
- may be difficult to return flowers
- foliage limited

Florists' shops

Advantages
- good range of flowers with long stems
- choice of foliage often available
- flowers can be returned if sub standard
- ability to send flowers easily through a relay service such as Interflora or EFlorist
- bespoke packaging
- service

Disadvantage
- flowers can be slightly more expensive than buying from a stall or supermarket

Major flower markets

Advantages
- can be less expensive
- vast range of product with longer stems
- good range of foliage

Disadvantages
- may have to buy in larger quantities than required
- unless you are a regular, valued customer it may prove difficult to return sub standard flowers
- you need to understand the product to get the best quality

Buying online

Advantages
- easy to purchase
- quality usually high

Disadvantages
- I prefer to see flowers rather than buying blind
- limited options
- you will be paying for the wrapping, which may not be needed if you want to arrange flowers
- foliage limited

General tips when purchasing

- Leaves should be a healthy green, not yellow.
- Double-headed flowers usually last longer than their single-headed counterparts such as single and double *Eustoma* (lisianthus) and *Freesia*.
- Loose pollen on petals is an indication that the flowers are nearing the end of their life.
- Flowers are vulnerable to draughts, so choose bunches that have been displayed inside the shop.
- Some cut flowers such as carnations and chrysanthemums live longer than others. Do not expect *Iris*, sweet peas or stocks to last as long.
- As a rule of thumb, scented flowers have a shorter life as a cut flower.
- The florets that make up the disc at the centre of spray chrysanthemums and *Gerbera* should not have released their yellow pollen. The centre should be clearly visible. There should be no loose pollen.
- Some but not all flowers have a fragrance. What is worth remembering is that flowers give off more scent in a warm room and high perfume is a sign of freshness.
- Bulb flowers, such as daffodils, anemones and tulips, last longer in shallow, not deep, water but always ensure they have a good supply.

right Spring flowers – in this example *Hyacinthus* – will last longer in shallow water changed regularly. The same applies to other flowers, such as *Anemone*, *Narcissus* and *Tulipa*.

To make your budget go further you may want to try growing your own cut flowers. The flowers listed below are easy to grow in the smallest of plots in the garden or even cracks in the wall! They are useful 'flower arranging all-rounders':

Alchemilla mollis Lime green froths of flowers that spread in shady conditions – a flower arranger's delight.

Alstroemeria Easy to grow in a sunny site. Produces long-lasting flowers over an extensive period.

Dahlia They keep on flowering for months. They are short-lived once cut so best to pick them straight from the garden.

Hydrangea Expensive to buy all months of the year but very easy to grow. Take care not to cut all the blooms off in one year as most varieties only produce flowers on second-year stems.

Lathyrus I buy small plug plants rather than using seed for an impressing cutting display in the summer.

Lavendula Incredibly easy to grow and thrives on exposed sunny sites. Select a blue rather than a grey variety when choosing for arranging.

Paeonia Beautiful but expensive flowers produced abundantly on well-established garden shrubs.

Rosa A garden rose offers a fragrance which is rarely matched by those from the florist.

Sedum Easy to grow and produces long-lasting flowers through summer to the late frosts.

Tulipa Tulips can be purchased very inexpensively so I love to grow more unusual varieties such as the large French tulips or the tiny species varities.

Valeriana This plant will grow in any corner of a small garden and can almost be described as a weed. It produces flowers for virtually every month of the year. Be careful though – it can spread prodigiously.

Using the flower A–Z

On the following pages there is an alphabetical listing of flowers suitable for flower arranging. Each entry is formatted as below to help you make the right choice.

botanical name

common name

Craspedia globosa
(Billy buttons)

Small gold-yellow flowering heads on sturdy long stems which dry extremely well. I prefer to purchase stems which are still slightly green and not totally grey. There should be no pollen on the flower heads or grey mould.

things to look out for

SPR	SUM	AUT	WIN
FORM	ROUND		

The form of each flower is listed – line, round or spray. Where the shape changes on opening both shapes are listed. Where a flower is a spray but round when the secondary stems are removed they also have the two categories.

The coloured boxes show the season where they are most readily available at the best price.

To learn more about form turn to page 72 in *Chapter 3: The Elements and Principles of Design*.

Acacia (mimosa)

The fluffy fragrant heads of mimosa usually have cellophane protection. Without this the flowers will dry out quickly. If on inspection they look dry do not buy. Make sure that some of the buds have burst into flower.

SPR	SUM	AUT	WIN
FORM	SPRAY		

Achillea (yarrow)

Achillea filipendulina can be easily grown in the garden or purchased from the florist. It dries well on the stem so if you are looking for fresher flowers search for stems that are greener rather than brown. The tiny flowers making up the bloom should not be crushed or broken. *A. millefolium* is available in more gentle colours than *A. filipendulina* – cream, pink and lemon – and the stems and flowers are not as robust.

SPR	SUM	AUT	WIN
FORM	ROUND		

Aconitum (monkshood)

A very poisonous flower, so avoid if you have small children. Do not use in table designs close to food and wash your hands after handling. Check that the flowers are evenly distributed along the stem and that there is no mildew on the leaves.

SPR	SUM	AUT	WIN
FORM	LINE		

Agapanthus (African lily)

These majestic flowers, in blue, white or cream, should have a few flowers opening on each stem. Check that the stem fully supports the flower. Gently turn upside down on purchasing to see how many flowers fall.

SPR	SUM	AUT	WIN
FORM	ROUND		

Alchemilla mollis (lady's mantle)

A delightful lime-green flower that is perfect with any bouquet of mixed flowers. Grow it in your garden in a shady spot and it will spread. If purchasing check that the flowers are not too tight as they may not fully develop.

SPR	SUM	AUT	WIN
FORM	SPRAY		

Allium (onion)

The ball of flowers should not be crushed. When purchasing, check that the water is clean as bacteria spread rapidly. *Allium* has a pungent onion smell that is stronger as it matures.

SPR	SUM	AUT	WIN
FORM	ROUND		

Alstroemeria
(Peruvian lily)

The flowers last for a long time (up to three weeks) and are usually purchased in bud. Check that the flowers are not too small as this means they have been cut when immature and will not develop fully. I like to buy *Alstroemeria* from a florist when at least one of the buds on each stem has burst. The foliage should be green not yellow and the leaves high up the stem should be intact. They are easily damaged and are sometimes removed.

SPR	SUM	AUT	WIN
FORM	SPRAY		

Amaranthus
(love-lies-bleeding)

Either upright or pendulous the *Amaranthus* is available in green, red or ginger brown. Check that the colour of the flowers is strong and not faded and that there is some foliage on the stem. Avoid if there is a lot of pollen drop.

SPR	SUM	AUT	WIN
FORM	LINE		

Ananas comosus
(ornamental pineapple)

The tips of the bracts at the top of the fruit should not be bent or dried but look fresh with a good tinge of green.

SPR	SUM	AUT	WIN
FORM	ROUND		

Anemone

Anemones last longer than many people think but avoid purchasing those that have powdery dark pollen on their petals. Check the stems are strong and not broken. They should not curl back excessively at the stem end. The foliage close to the head of the flower should not be drying out. If it is, submerge under water for a few minutes to give it a new lease of life.

SPR	SUM	AUT	WIN
FORM	ROUND		

Anigozanthos
(kangaroo paw)

A weed in Australia but prized as a cut flower in other parts of the world. One or two of the florets on each stem should be open on purchase. Check that the lower flowers are not shrivelled at the base of the flowering stem. *Anigozanthos* will dry out quickly if they do not have a regular supply of water.

SPR	SUM	AUT	WIN
FORM	SPRAY		

Anthurium
(flamingo flower)

Avoid purchasing *Anthurium* with a crease or blemish as this will become more dominant and turn brown very quickly. The top third of the spadix should be smooth and the tip must not be brown. No pollen should have been released. Take care when handling the spathes.

SPR	SUM	AUT	WIN
FORM	ROUND		

Antirrhinum (snapdragon)

Purchase stems that are not bent at the flowering tips as they will never straighten. There should be a good show of flowers at the bottom of the stem. The stems should be strong with leaves that are not crushed.

SPR (late)	SUM	AUT	WIN
FORM	LINE		

Asclepias (butterfly weed)

If the flowers are in tight bud they will not develop fully and go limp quickly. The stems contain a milky sap which is an irritant. Hold the stem ends in a flame so they seal and prevent leakage.

SPR	SUM	AUT	WIN
FORM	SPRAY		

Aster (Michaelmas daisy)

I prefer stems that have long secondary stems with numerous flowers and crisp foliage.

SPR	SUM	AUT	WIN
FORM	SPRAY		

Astilbe

A water-loving plant that dries out quickly. Check that the leaves are not curling or the tips wilting through lack of moisture.

SPR	SUM	AUT	WIN
FORM	LINE		

Astrantia (masterwort)

The flowers will wilt if the stem has been cut when immature. They should be open and the stems strong. They will then dry to perfection.

SPR	SUM	AUT	WIN
FORM	SPRAY		

Bouvardia

Purchase only top-quality grades with at least one of the flower heads on each stem starting to open. Inferior grades with small tight flowers will not develop and wilt quickly.

SPR	SUM	AUT	WIN
FORM	SPRAY		

Brassica
(ornamental cabbage)

Check that the centre of the *Brassica* is not sprouting and is more or less level with the outer leaves. The water should not have an unpleasant odour.

SPR	SUM	AUT	WIN
FORM	ROUND		

Bupleurum

Classified as both foliage and a flower. Buy if the yellow/green flowers are well developed on strong, non-tangled stems.

SPR	SUM	AUT	WIN
FORM	SPRAY		

Calendula officialis
(pot marigold)

I like the marigold to be flat-headed rather than raised in the centre. The petals should not be crushed.

SPR	SUM	AUT	WIN
FORM	ROUND		

Campanula (bellflower)

The flowers on the spike do not need to be open on purchase but the buds should look full and ready to open. The stem ends should be clean and not mushy.

SPR	SUM	AUT	WIN
FORM	LINE		

Carthamus tinctorius
(safflower)

Carthamus can be purchased in orange (the colour has long been used as a dye) or in cream. The orange has more impact. The heads should be fluffy and there should be a good number on each spray – a minimum of three heads. *Carthamus* dries well and keeps its colour.

SPR	SUM	AUT	WIN
FORM	SPRAY		

Celosia

Celosia cristata is fan-shaped or round-headed and *Celosia* Plumosa Group is pointed. *Celosia* is susceptible to botrytis so check there are no brown marks on the flower, particularly on *C. cristata*.

SPR	SUM	AUT	WIN
FORM	LINE or ROUND		

Chamelaucium (waxflower)

This can be purchased open or in bud.
I prefer the open flower as the bud version
will not develop further once cut. A few of
the flowers may drop when unwrapped but
this is not a problem.

SPR	SUM	AUT	WIN
FORM	SPRAY		

Chrysanthemum

When purchasing spray chrysanthemums
you may wish to choose those with long
secondary stems which can be used
individually in a small design. When
purchasing single-headed 'bloom'
chrysanthemums check there is no sign of
browning at the centre of the flower or on
the stem at the base of the flower.
If there is, the flower is likely to shatter.

SPR	SUM	AUT	WIN
FORM	ROUND or SPRAY		

Convallaria (lily-of-the-valley)

As the flowers get older they go brown
from the bottom.

SPR	SUM	AUT	WIN
FORM	LINE		

Craspedia globosa (Billy buttons)

Small gold-yellow flowering heads on sturdy
long stems which dry extremely well. I prefer
to purchase stems which are still slightly
green and not totally grey. There should be
no pollen on the flower heads or grey mould.

SPR	SUM	AUT	WIN
FORM	ROUND		

Crocosmia (montbretia)

The racemes of *Crocosmia* can be
purchased green or orange-red. I feel the
orange-yellow flowers give more for the
money. The buds should be full.

SPR	SUM	AUT	WIN
FORM	LINE		

Dahlia

Check that the outer petals are firm, not
shrivelled, and the foliage is crisp. The
centre of the flowers should be very tight.

SPR	SUM	AUT	WIN
FORM	ROUND		

Delphinium

Check that the foliage is not damaged and is not looking sad. The flowers at the bottom of the stem should be fresh and not wilted.

SPR	SUM	AUT	WIN
FORM	LINE		

Dianthus (bloom carnation)

For preference buy carnations in open bud rather than fully open. If you wish to have fuller blooms tease out the petals of the bud with your fingers and like magic you will have a fuller form. If the filament and stamens can be seen in the centre then the flower will be older rather than younger.

SPR	SUM	AUT	WIN
FORM	ROUND		

Dianthus (spray carnation)

Avoid flowers that have split or brown calyces at the base of the flower. Purchase spray carnations that show colour in at least three buds on the stem. If the bud does not show colour it is unlikely to open.

SPR	SUM	AUT	WIN
FORM	SPRAY		

Dianthus barbatus (sweet William)

A long-lasting, scented flower that is great value for money. I prefer to buy those where at least two flowers have burst on each stem rather than all being still in bud. Check there is no mildew on the leaves.

SPR	SUM	AUT	WIN
FORM	ROUND		

Eremurus (foxtail lily)

These tall flowers open slowly from the bottom upwards. The spent flowers at the base of the stem should be removed. If a lot of these are missing the stock is old.

SPR	SUM	AUT	WIN
FORM	LINE		

Eryngium (sea holly)

Try and find *Eryngium* with crisp leaves and petals.

SPR	SUM	AUT	WIN
FORM	SPRAY		

Euphorbia

Old stock often has the leaves removed as they go limp quite quickly. Check that the flowers look vibrant and that those at the stem end are not shrivelled. Take care as you prepare the flowers as the latex sap is poisonous. Burn the stem ends to seal.

SPR	SUM	AUT	WIN
FORM	LINE		

Eustoma (lisianthus)

The purple/blue lisianthus is particularly susceptible to botrytis – a brown discolouring of the petals which spreads rapidly. Do check that there are no marks on the flowers you purchase. If the young buds at the top have bent stems they will not straighten.

SPR	SUM	AUT	WIN
FORM	ROUND or SPRAY		

Freesia

Freesia should have plump buds and one flower open or on the point of opening. If the raceme appears too elongated you can remove the tiny top buds. They will not open and removing them stimulates the opening of buds further down the stem.

SPR	SUM	AUT	WIN
FORM	LINE		

Genista (broom)

Try to purchase the first cutting of broom; the second tends to be on hard wood that is more difficult to arrange. *Genista* has a lovely gentle fragrance. If the bunch is too tightly bound check that there is no mould at the base of the flowering stems. When unwrapped expect a few flowers to drop. This is acceptable.

SPR	SUM	AUT	WIN
FORM	SPRAY		

Gentiana (gentian)

A lovely blue spike of glorious blue but make sure that the buds are full – they do not really develop further once purchased.

SPR	SUM	AUT	WIN
FORM	LINE		

Gerbera and mini Gerbera (germini)

The centre of the flowers should be clean with no loose pollen. I prefer stems that do not narrow considerably towards the head. The narrowing of the stem means that water has more difficulty reaching the flower. *Gerbera* are very susceptible to bacteria so add one drop of bleach to a large vase of water when you get them home. Place in shallow not deep water as the tiny hairs on the stem will get waterlogged and soften the stem.

SPR	SUM	AUT	WIN
FORM	ROUND		

Gladiolus

Remove the tips from gladioli. They will not open and removing them stimulates the buds further down the stem to open. Crisp leaves indicate freshness.

SPR	SUM	AUT	WIN
FORM	LINE		

Gloriosa superba (glory lily)

Gloriosa are sold in special bags to cushion them against damage. Leave them in the bag until you are ready to use them. There should be no spotting on the petals and the colour should be vibrant, not dull or transparent. Those that have a volumetric rather than a flat form last longer.

SPR	SUM	AUT	WIN
FORM	ROUND		

Gomphocarpus physocarpus

The stem bears hairy bags full of air. Check that these are not squashed.

SPR	SUM	AUT	WIN
FORM	LINE		

Gypsophila (baby's breath)

As *Gypsophila* gets older it tends to smell and get tangled so go for a pleasant fragrance and easy-to-work stems. If you are buying a wrap look inside the cellophane or paper to the centre and check that it is not brown at the base. If the flowers are starting to go brown it will not last. Fresh *Gypsophila* will be heavier than older *Gypsophila* that has started to dry out. I like to purchase when at least half the flowers are open as often they do not develop greatly once cut.

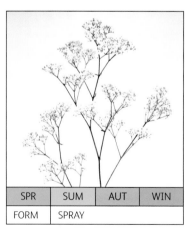

SPR	SUM	AUT	WIN
FORM	SPRAY		

Helianthus (sunflower)

Avoid heads that are very large as their weight makes them difficult to position in foam. If the flowers look tight do not worry as they usually open. Avoid purchasing flowers with loose pollen at the centre. Retain some leaves near the head to pull water up the stems more easily.

SPR	SUM	AUT	WIN
FORM	ROUND		

Heliconia

There are many different *Heliconia* but the one illustrated is also known as lobster claw. Small true flowers are contained within the colourful, waxy, sturdy bracts. Avoid stems where the flowers cannot be seen and with a lot of brown marks. The bracts should have good colour and not be brown/black and spotted.

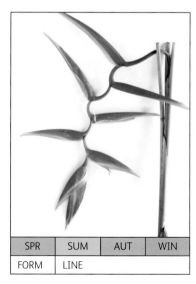

SPR	SUM	AUT	WIN
FORM	LINE		

Helleborus (hellebore)

Hellebores are now available for purchase as a cut flower. If the seedcase is well formed in the centre and the stamens have lost their pollen they will last well and can be used in foam; otherwise use only in water.

SPR	SUM	AUT	WIN
FORM	ROUND		

Hippeastrum (amaryllis)

Amaryllis have hollow stems which curl back on to themselves under water. Recut the stem ends daily. You can tie a length of florist's tape or wool or wrap a rubber band around the stem close to the end. If the flowers are open and you can see the pollen they are not fresh.

SPR	SUM	AUT	WIN
FORM	ROUND		

Hyacinthus

At least the top two-thirds of the spike of flowers should be tight. Keep the bulbous white ends of the hyacinth on the stem as these contain food that feeds the flowering heads.

SPR	SUM	AUT	WIN
FORM	LINE		

Hydrangea

Choose *Hydrangea* heads that have firm, almost crisp petal-like sepals. If they wilt, submerge their heads in tepid water for 30 minutes. This treatment can revive them but only if the wilt is not extreme. The sepals can go transparent if under water for too long a period. Prevent them from wilting by gently spraying with water.
I prefer to purchase *Hydrangea* that have been cut on brown wood from the previous year (the current year's growth is green) as they usually last longer.

SPR	SUM	AUT	WIN
FORM	ROUND		

Hypericum (St John's wort)

The berries should be plump with bright green calyces. There should be no black berries on the stem as this is a sign of ageing. If there is a smell of 'curry' the berries are too mature.

SPR	SUM	AUT	WIN
FORM	SPRAY		

Iris

Even the highest-quality *Iris* will not last a week. It is a glorious short-lived flower and should be purchased in the pencil form to gain the most from its life. I prefer a touch of colour to be showing in the flowers then you can be sure they will open. Check there is no dryness at the edges of the flowers or leaves.

SPR	SUM	AUT	WIN
FORM	LINE or ROUND		

Ixia (corn lily)

Healthy stems are green without brown marks. Select stems where a couple of the lower flowers are open.

SPR	SUM	AUT	WIN
FORM	LINE		

Kniphofia (red hot poker)

The flower opens from the bottom upwards so check that the florets at the bottom of the flowering head are not spent. The stems should be strong and the ends not mushy.

SPR	SUM	AUT	WIN
FORM	LINE		

Lathyrus (sweet pea)

The buds at the top of the flower should show colour. The flowers at the base die first so check that those at the base are not crêpey and limp and that they do not drop when very gently shaken.

SPR	SUM	AUT	WIN
FORM	LINE		

Lavendula (lavender)

Purchase when the flowers are developed. They will not really develop any further once cut. If packed tightly together check there is no mould at the base of the bunch. English lavender is greyer blue than the typical French lavender. The English usually has more fragrance.

SPR	SUM	AUT	WIN
FORM	LINE		

Leucadendron

The green *Leucadendron* and the red variety *L.* 'Safari Sunset' are long- lasting flowers. The attractive leaves should hide the inconspicuous central flower if fresh. The centre becomes exposed in an older flower. Purchase stems that are straight.

SPR	SUM	AUT	WIN
FORM	LINE		

Leucospermum

This member of the *Protea* family will last well but I prefer to purchase those that do not have a fluffy grey mass at the centre – it is simply a question of choosing the right variety. Make sure the tough leaves have a greenish tinge to ensure their freshness and that the stems are strong enough to support the size of the head. Quality stems are straight. The stamens rising from the mass of individual flowers at the base should be vertical and not bending outwards.

SPR	SUM	AUT	WIN
FORM	ROUND		

Liatris

Check that the foliage and stem are a fresh green and not dull green or black and mushy. Unusually this flower opens from the top downwards. I prefer to buy when about 15 per cent of the flowers are open. Check there is no mould at the centre of the bunch if tightly packed together and/or black leaves and stems.

Lilium

Do not buy lilies which have had the stamens cut out to prevent them shedding pollen. It also spoils the look of this gracious flower. Avoid lily heads where the petals are opening individually rather than all at the same time. Lilies will open only when they are ready. Despite much experimentation, I have found no guaranteed way of hurrying the process. If they are for an occasion, buy them at least five days in advance in the summer and 7–12 days in advance in the winter. Buy lilies with a strong stem. If a stem flops when you hold it close to the end, the growth has been too quick and will hold the open flower heads only with difficulty. The foliage should be green with no signs of yellowing. Do remember that all lilies are poisonous to cats if eaten.

Limonium (statice)

An everlasting flower that needs to be purchased when the flowers are open as they will not develop further once cut. The foliage should be crisp and not limp.

SPR	SUM	AUT	WIN
FORM	LINE or SPRAY		

SPR	SUM	AUT	WIN
FORM	LINE		

SPR	SUM	AUT	WIN
FORM	ROUND or SPRAY		

Lysimachia (loosestrife)

Purchase only if about one-third of the flowers are open otherwise it may have been cut when too immature. The stems should be strong and straight and the leaves should look robust and show no signs of yellowing.

Matthiola (Brompton stocks)

Purchase when the top flowers on the spike are in bud and the lowest flowers open. Remove most of the leaves from the stocks before cutting the stem ends. The leaves are lush and fleshy and will take the water needed in the flowering head.

Moluccella laevis (bells of Ireland)

The group of bracts at the top of the stem should be intact and not have been removed. The actual flower of *Moluccella* is white and inconspicuous, often hidden by the lime-green calyces. Check that the stamens of the white flowers are not prominent and droopy. The calyces should be a bright lively green and the stems should be strong and not bent.

SPR	SUM	AUT	WIN
FORM	LINE		

SPR	SUM	AUT	WIN
FORM	LINE		

SPR	SUM	AUT	WIN
FORM	LINE		

Muscari (grape hyacinth)

Easy-to-grow garden flower that spreads rapidly but if purchasing check that the higher bells are tightly closed and the lower bells are not shrivelled and darker in hue. The bottom of the stems should not be mushy.

SPR	SUM	AUT	WIN
FORM	LINE		

Narcissus

All *Narcissus*, such as the daffodil and the smaller *N.* 'Tête à tête', have a sap in their stems that is poisonous to other flowers. Consequently they should not be mixed with any other flowers. Wipe away the sap before arranging and they will last longer.

SPR	SUM	AUT	WIN
FORM	LINE or ROUND		

Nerine (Guernsey lily)

These are now available in white, red and peach as well as the classic pink. As the flowers are volumetric they are easily crushed so it is better to purchase when the flowers are only slightly open.

SPR	SUM	AUT	WIN
FORM	SPRAY		

Orchid – Cymbidium

The *Cymbidium* orchid is terrific value most months of the year except July and August. Check how many flowers are on the stem – it can range from 8 to 16. The size varies from mini to maxi and this also determines the price. If the end of the stem is in a plastic tube check there is water in the tube. Look at the petals on the flowers. If they curve outwards they tend to be more mature than if they curve inwards.
A crêpey look to the petals means that the flowers are old. Check there is no brown on the stems or petals.

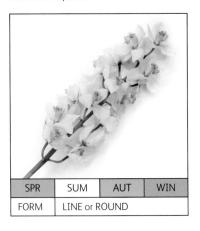

SPR	SUM	AUT	WIN
FORM	LINE or ROUND		

Orchid – Dendrobium (Singapore orchid, Florida orchid)

Check that the flowers are not showing signs of being transparent as this is an indication of age. The flowers drop from the bottom so if in packaging gently shake to see if any flowers fall. They can be purchased in phials of water or with cotton wool around the stem ends. Those in phials are often of superior quality. Check there is water in the phial.

SPR	SUM	AUT	WIN
FORM	LINE		

Orchid – Phalaenopsis (moth orchid)

As a cut flower the *Phalaenopsis* usually consists of open flowers rather than buds (which are commonly seen on the pot plant). Check how many blooms are on the stem as this can vary considerably. The petals of the flowers should not be transparent as this is an indication of an older flower.

SPR	SUM	AUT	WIN
FORM	LINE or ROUND		

Orchid – Vanda

Blue is the colour normally associated with the *Vanda* but they are now available in pink, dark purple, red, white and even orange and sandy-brown. *Vanda* is an expensive flower and the cost is usually based on the number of blooms on the stem. They can look droopy when in fact they are not! If submerged under water they last well.

SPR	SUM	AUT	WIN
FORM	LINE or ROUND		

Origanum vulgare (marjoram)

This sweet-smelling herb needs to be strong and fragrant. Check that it has not been kept in deep water as the stems will be slimy and the leaves waterlogged. The purple flowers should have colour but it is a subtle not a showy flower.

SPR	SUM	AUT	WIN
FORM	SPRAY		

Ornithogalum (chincherinchee, Star of Bethlehem)

Ornithogalum arabicum has a rounder shape and *O. thyrsoides* is more linear. This is an incredibly long-lasting flower. Purchase when a couple of the buds have burst into flower. Check that there is no slime on the stems – this usually occurs at the bottom of the stem.

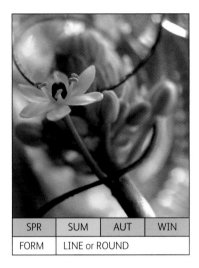

SPR	SUM	AUT	WIN
FORM	LINE or ROUND		

Paeonia (peony)

Choose peonies that are showing some colour on the bud. If the bud is too tight it may be a sign that the flower was picked prematurely and it may never open. Conversely, once fully open they will last only a few days. If you wish to keep your peonies from opening, store them in a box out of water in a cool place, where they can be kept for up to five days without harm. They will open once they are placed in water.

SPR (late)	SUM (early)	AUT	WIN
FORM	ROUND		

Papaver (poppy)

Poppies are usually sold covered with cellophane to avoid dehydration. The buds should show colour but avoid purchasing open flowers as their life is short. The stems contain latex, which is an irritant. After cutting, seal in a flame to prevent the latex leaking. They are so beautiful it is worth it!

SPR	SUM	AUT	WIN
FORM	ROUND		

Phlox

A charming long-lasting flower if you purchase stems with open flowers and lots of buds. The mature flowers will drop but the buds will continue to open over a long period.

SPR	SUM	AUT	WIN
FORM	SPRAY		

Physalis (Chinese lanterns)

Physalis are available in green or orange. If purchasing the orange seedheads make sure that the colour is evident in most of the lanterns. The lanterns should not be squashed. If they are you can blow into them and they will regain their shape.

SPR	SUM	AUT	WIN
FORM	LINE		

Polianthes (tuberose)

This highly perfumed flower should be purchased when most of the flowers are still in bud. There should be no brown on the petals and the stems should be sturdy.

SPR	SUM	AUT	WIN
FORM	LINE		

Polygonatum (Solomon's seal)

Polygonatum is very susceptible to damage from leaf-eating insects so check that there are no holes in the leaves. The leaves should be strong and rise proud of the flowers.

SPR	SUM	AUT	WIN
FORM	LINE		

Protea

There should be no brown marks on the green leaves or bracts surrounded the flower. It is often easier to work with stems that are straighter.

SPR	SUM	AUT	WIN
FORM	ROUND		

Prunus (cherry blossom)

Prunus branches are available in various lengths. Check that the buds are not too tight as they will not develop. If the flowers are too mature they will fall copiously if the stem is gently shaken.

SPR	SUM	AUT	WIN
FORM	LINE		

Ranunculus (turban flower)

Purchase in bud and allow the flower to develop in a vase. *Ranunculus* are not happy in foam. Remove most of the leaves from the stems as they rot very quickly and place in a vase with space between the stems. There is a new variety called 'Cloni' which is more than double the size of the classic *Ranunculus*.

SPR	SUM	AUT	WIN
FORM	ROUND		

Rosa

Fresh roses are firm to squeeze at the widest part of the head. Do not purchase those with brown marks on the petals. If the stems are severely bent they are usually seconds. If the top leaves are far from the head, say more than 10 cm (4 in), it could be that the flower has grown too quickly or too close to others. They will not be as strong. Roses from Ecuador and Colombia are becoming very popular as their head sizes are very large.

SPR	SUM	AUT	WIN
FORM	ROUND		

Rosa (spray)

Spray roses should have at least three buds on a stem showing good colour. Evenly spaced, undamaged foliage on the stem is a sign of quality.

SPR	SUM	AUT	WIN
FORM	SPRAY		

Scabiosa

Available in pink. white and burgundy but most commonly blue, this delightful summer flower dries out quickly. It needs to be kept in a cool position and purchased when the centre of the flower is tight and the flowers are open, not in bud. The leaves should be in good condition.

SPR	SUM	AUT	WIN
FORM	ROUND		

Sedum (ice plant)

A plant that is easy to grow in the garden and spreads quickly. When purchasing check that the leaves are a strong green as they yellow with age. The head should form a compact mass of colour – pink or white.

SPR	SUM	AUT	WIN
FORM	SPRAY		

Solidago (golden rod)

Available for purchase in several grades. I always buy the premium grade, where many of the flowers are open rather than in bud. The same applies to x *Solidaster* (which has slightly larger more open flowers). Flowers that are not open on purchase will rarely open.

SPR	SUM	AUT	WIN
FORM	SPRAY		

Stephanotis

Stephanotis is a valued wedding flower as it has a lovely waxy texture and lasts well out of water. Heads are usually sold in a plastic bag. They should not show signs of bruising or be tinged with brown. They should have a strong fragrance.

SPR	SUM	AUT	WIN
FORM	SPRAY		

Strelitzia (bird-of-paradise)

One bright colourful flower should be evident on purchase. You may not be aware but in every bract sheath, there is at least one more flower. This will not emerge unless it is prised open. The sheath therefore needs to be plump.

SPR	SUM	AUT	WIN
FORM	DIFFICULT ONE!		

Symphoricarpos (snowberry)

In white or pink this long-lasting berry is lovely in late autumn designs. Check that the berries are plump and not shrivelled or turning brown.

SPR	SUM	AUT	WIN
FORM	SPRAY		

Syringa (lilac)

Remove all the foliage before cutting the stem at a sharp angle and placing in water. Add cut shrub food if you have this available.

SPR	SUM	AUT	WIN
FORM	LINE or SPRAY		

Trachelium

Trachelium can be purchased in purple, white or green but purple *Trachelium* is most widely available. Check that the colour looks fresh and that the flowers do not look tired around the edge and have not been squashed. The leaves are relatively inconspicuous but they should not be limp.

SPR	SUM	AUT	WIN
FORM	ROUND		

Tulipa

When selecting tulips, look for bunches where the leaves are level or higher than the flower heads. Once cut, the flower heads continue to grow at a much faster rate than the leaves.

SPR	SUM	AUT	WIN
FORM	LINE or ROUND		

Veronica

Veronica needs to be strong, so the best quality is the one that will last. Avoid *Veronica* that looks floppy. It likes lots of water and a cool room.

SPR	SUM	AUT	WIN
FORM	LINE		

Viburnum opulus 'Roseum' (guelder rose, snowball)

Treat as for *Syringa* (lilac). I do, however, like to leave the top two leaves around each bloom. The small flowers that create each bloom should not be too tight as they need to be relatively mature in order to fully open and last.

SPR	SUM	AUT	WIN
FORM	SPRAY		

Viburnum tinus (laurustinus)

Viburnum tinus can be purchased in either flowering or berry form. If purchasing the flowering form, some of the buds on each bloom should have burst. If all the flowers are in bud they will not develop further once cut from the shrub. When purchasing the blue-black berry form I prefer to buy stems where the berries are tightly packed together rather than loosely arrayed.

SPR	SUM	AUT	WIN
FORM	SPRAY		

Zantedeschia (calla lily, arum lily)

Avoid purchasing *Zantedeschia* that has a lot of pollen on the flower. The stems of calla lilies produce a lot of bacteria so make sure you change the water regularly. Place *Zantedeschia* in shallow, not deep water as with all bulb flowers.

SPR	SUM	AUT	WIN
FORM	LINE		

A–Z OF FOLIAGE

Foliage that is easy to grow or purchase from the florist

Here you will find illustrated a wide range of foliage that I find particularly useful in flower design. Some of the foliage has fruits and/or flowers in addition, and others listed may just be for the stems, such as *Cornus* and *Equisetum*. I have specified in most cases the particular type of plant shown, but for easy reference the first part of the title e.g. *Camellia* will be sufficient. Where the use of a common name is widespread this is in brackets after the botanical name.

Foliage that is more commonly found in the garden is highlighted in a green box.

GARDEN

Where the foliage is usually purchased from the florist this is highlighted in a purple box.

FLORIST

Of course many have the two symbols.

GARDEN	FLORIST

Using the foliage A–Z

You will find on the following pages an alphabetic listing of some of the most useful foliage in flower arranging. The listing uses the botanical names together with any well-known common name. Each entry is formatted as below for easy reference.

botanical name   common name

➤ *Fatsia japonica* 'Variegata' (variegated aralia) ◄

↗ FLORIST	GARDEN ↘

foliage is available to buy from a florist

this means that the foliage is commonly found in the garden

Abelia

GARDEN

Asparagus densiflorus 'Myersii' (foxtail fern)

FLORIST

Asparagus setaceus (asparagus fern)

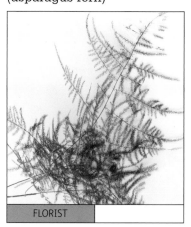

FLORIST

Asparagus umbellatus (ming fern)

FLORIST

Asparagus virgatus (tree fern)

FLORIST

Aspidistra elatior (cast iron plant)

FLORIST | GARDEN

Asplenium

FLORIST

Aucuba japonica (spotted laurel)

GARDEN

Bergenia cordifolia (elephant's ears)

GARDEN

Bupleurum griffithii

FLORIST	

Buxus
(box)

FLORIST	GARDEN

Calathea roseopicta

FLORIST	

Camellia

FLORIST	GARDEN

Choisya ternata
(Mexican orange blossom)

	GARDEN

Cocculus

FLORIST	

Codiaeum
(croton)

FLORIST	

Cordyline fruticosa

FLORIST	

Cornus sericea 'Flaviramea'
(yellow dogwood)

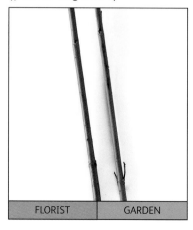

FLORIST	GARDEN

Corylus avellana 'Contorta'
(corkscrew hazel)

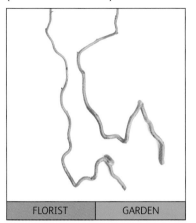

FLORIST	GARDEN

Costus stenophyllus
(lipstick)

FLORIST	

Cotinus coggygria 'Royal Purple' (smoke bush)

FLORIST	GARDEN

Cyperus alternifolius
(umbrella plant)

FLORIST	

Cytisus
(broom)

FLORIST	GARDEN

Danae racemosa
(soft ruscus)

FLORIST	GARDEN

Daphne

FLORIST	GARDEN

Dracaena sanderiana 'Victory'

FLORIST	

Elaeagnus pungens 'Maculata'

	GARDEN

Epimedium

GARDEN

Equisetum hyemale
(snakegrass)

FLORIST

Escallonia

GARDEN

Eucalyptus 'Baby Blue'

FLORIST

Eucalyptus cinerea

FLORIST

Eucalyptus parvifolia

FLORIST

Eucalyptus populus
(fruiting eucalyptus)

FLORIST

Euonymus japonicus

GARDEN

Euphorbia
(spurge or old John)

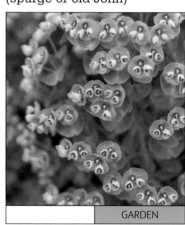

GARDEN

Fagus
(beech)

FLORIST	GARDEN

Fatsia japonica
(aralia)

FLORIST	GARDEN

Fatsia japonica 'Variegata'
(variegated aralia)

FLORIST	GARDEN

Galax urceolata
(beetleweed)

FLORIST	

Gardenia

FLORIST	

Garrya elliptica

	GARDEN

Gaultheria shallon
(salal, lemon leaf)

FLORIST	

Grevillea longifolia
(fernleaf grevillea)

FLORIST	

Griselinia littoralis

	GARDEN

Hebe rakaiensis
(veronica)

FLORIST	GARDEN

Hedera arborescens
(tree ivy, with berries)

FLORIST	GARDEN

Hedera helix
(ivy trails)

FLORIST	GARDEN

Heuchera

	GARDEN

Hosta
(funkia)

FLORIST	GARDEN

Howea
(Phoenix palm)

FLORIST	

Ilex
(holly)

FLORIST	GARDEN

Laurus nobilis
(bay laurel, sweet bay)

FLORIST	GARDEN

Ligustrum
(privet)

FLORIST	GARDEN

Magnolia grandiflora
(bull bay)

	GARDEN

Monstera deliciosa
(Swiss cheese plant)

FLORIST	GARDEN

Myrtus
(myrtle)

FLORIST	GARDEN

Pandanus baptistii
(screw pine)

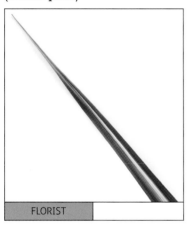

FLORIST	

Parthenocissus tricuspidata

	GARDEN

Philodendron erubescens
(blushing philodendron)

FLORIST	

Philodendron 'Xanadu'

FLORIST	

Phormium tenax
(New Zealand flax)

FLORIST	GARDEN

Photinia x *fraseri* 'Red Robin'
(red top, red tip)

FLORIST	GARDEN

Physocarpus

GARDEN

**Pittosporum
tenuifolium**

FLORIST GARDEN

**Pittosporum
tobira**

FLORIST

**Pittosporum heterophyllum
variegata** (tondo)

FLORIST

Polypodium punctatum
(deer's horn fern)

FLORIST

Polystichum setiferum
(fern)

FLORIST GARDEN

Prunus laurocerasus
(cherry laurel)

FLORIST GARDEN

Prunus lusitanicia
(Portuguese laurel)

FLORIST GARDEN

Rhapis excelsa
(lady palm)

FLORIST

Rhododendron ponticum
(common rhododendron)

FLORIST	GARDEN

Ribes sanguineum
(flowering currant)

	GARDEN

Rosmarinus

FLORIST	GARDEN

Rumohra adiantiformis
(leatherleaf)

FLORIST	

Ruscus hypophyllum
(hard ruscus)

FLORIST	

Salix
(pussy willow)

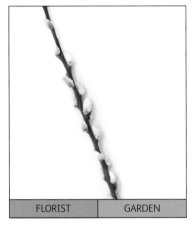

FLORIST	GARDEN

Sansevieria cylindrica

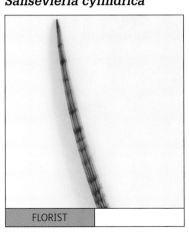

FLORIST	

Sansevieria trifasciata
(mother-in-law's tongue)

FLORIST	

Schoenus melanostachys
(flexi grass)

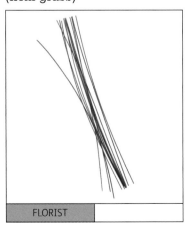

FLORIST	

Skimmia japonica

FLORIST	GARDEN

Sorbus aria
(whitebeam)

FLORIST	GARDEN

Sorbus aucuparia
(mountain ash or rowan)

	GARDEN

Stachys lanata
(lamb's ear)

FLORIST	GARDEN

Stitcherus flabellus
(umbrella fern)

FLORIST	

Viburnum tinus

FLORIST	GARDEN

Weigela florida
(evergreen weigela)

	GARDEN

Xanthorrhoea johnsonii
(steel grass)

FLORIST	

Xerophyllum tenax
(bear grass)

FLORIST	

CONDITIONING PLANT MATERIAL

To prolong the life of cut flowers and foliage, thus ensuring that they do not wilt prematurely, we 'condition' them.

To condition plant material

- First ensure that all your components and implements are spotlessly clean as plant material dies prematurely if bacteria enter the stem. Bacteria are produced on all that is dirty – be it water, buckets, containers, scissors, knives or secateurs.

- With a sharp pair of floral scissors, remove the bottom 10 per cent of the stem on a slant. Florists will usually use a sharp knife, but without experience efficient handling is difficult. This diagonal cut exposes the largest amount of the stem's inner tissue, which transports water to the flower heads and leaves. It also prevents the stem end from sealing. Cut just above a node (the knobbly bits from which the leaves grow, which occur at regular intervals along the stem). Cutting just below or on the nodes impedes water uptake.

- Remove any leaves that would be below the water line, because long-term submersion encourages bacterial growth.

- Place in a bucket of lukewarm water (the two exceptions to this rule are chrysanthemums and *Bouvardia*, which both need cool water). The water should be deep for strong-stemmed flowers, such as roses, and shallow for those with soft fleshy stems, such as daffodils, anemones and other bulb flowers.

- Once in water, leave the plant material in a cool place. A warm and dry atmosphere encourages water to evaporate through the leaves. Similarly, arrangements should be placed away from draughts, central heating, sunny window ledges and the heat emitted by televisions.

- If possible, collect flowers and foliage from the garden in the evening. By this time, the plant will have stored its maximum reserves of food for use during darkness. The cool of evening also means that little moisture is lost through the leaves by transpiration.

- The stems of certain plants, such as those in the spurge family (*Euphorbiaceae*), contain a milky sap called latex, which is an irritant. Take care not to touch the eyes or mouth after handling them. Once cut, hold the stem end briefly in a flame to prevent the sap from oozing out and blocking the stem entrance. If this procedure is not followed, water cannot enter the stem.

- Wash away any dirt from foliage by submerging it in water containing a drop of washing-up liquid. Do not submerge immature foliage for too long, but you can leave more mature leaves for up to an hour. Rinse the foliage well before using. Do not submerge silver or grey foliage, because the tiny hairs on the surface of the leaf become waterlogged and loose their 'greyness'.

- Ethylene gas, which is emitted by ripening fruit, vegetables and decaying plants, shortens the life of cut flowers. It is important, therefore, always to remove the dying heads on a flower spray and to keep flowers that are particularly susceptible – including carnations, *Gypsophila* and orchids – away from fruit and vegetables.

Making flowers last longer

Flowers bought from florists have usually been treated with a silver nitrate solution to retard the ageing process. This is why delicate blooms, including sweet peas, can now last for more than five days.

Tips and treatments that do work

Cut flower food
Sachets of cut flower food are provided by many florists and supermarkets to help your plant material to last longer and they really do work. The special formula prevents the rapid increase of bacteria and encourages the flowers and foliage to develop to their full potential. Do not change the water but add water containing more cut flower food.

Aspirin
Scientific research suggests that the acid in aspirin stimulates a plant's defence mechanism. Adding a small amount to the water may protect against bacteria.

Chrysal Glory® Spray
Glory is a trade product available in a spray can. If it is sprayed on to the fresh flowers, the flowers will last up to 50 per cent longer by reducing moisture loss. It really does work (refer to www.chrysal.com). You may have difficulty obtaining Glory as it is a trade product.

Leaf Shine
Spraying Leaf Shine on dark green strong leaves such as those of *Monstera* will make them last longer as well as look more glossy and cleaner. Spray outdoors and take care to follow the instructions on the can. Do not spray too heavily or the surface will appear to be greasy and will be difficult to remove. Sometimes it can mark the surface of the leaf, for example, black marks may appear on *Aspidistra* leaves. Leaf shine wipes are just as effective.

Ripening fruit
Do not place fresh flowers close to fruit as the ethylene gas given off by ripening fruit shortens the life of flowers.

Tips and treatments that do not work

Sugar or lemonade
Sugar is a food for bacteria as well as for flowers and therefore encourages them to multiply.

Smashing and hammering the stems
Do not hammer or smash the ends of stems. The ensuing damage to cell tissue encourages the rapid growth of bacteria and thus reduces the life of the plant material. If you are removing thorns from roses, take care not to damage the stem, as this would allow bacteria to enter.

Tip that might work! ?

Copper coins
As copper is a fungicide it is said to help prevent bacteria forming in the water. You could try putting a copper coin in the water.

How to revive a wilted rose

To revive a rose there are two treatments that seem
to work. I prefer method A.

NB A rose will revive only if it has wilted prematurely.
These methods will not revive a dead rose.

Method A

1 Remove at least the bottom 10 per cent of the stem as this is where the blockage usually occurs.

2 Place the stem horizontally in a basin or bowl of deep water.

3 Leave the rose for an hour and it could well have revived.

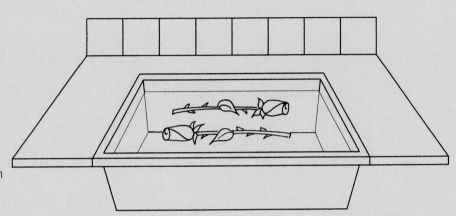

Method B

1 Remove at least the bottom 10 per cent of the stem as this is where the blockage usually occurs.

2 Place the bottom 5 cm (2 in) of the stem in a mug or bucket holding very hot water for 60 seconds. If the flower is delicate place a paper bag over the head to keep off the steam.

3 Remove from the hot water and place the stem in deeper tepid water. Leave in a cool place for several hours.

$\mathcal{M}$echanics means the equipment that will keep your stems in place. Floral foam, chicken wire and pinholders are the most traditional mediums, but with changes in the floral scene decorative wire, ribbon, sticks, tape, test tubes, gravel, beads and shells are also used to enable greater diversity of design.

Floral sundries are tools that make arranging easier. In this chapter I describe the ones that I consider most useful and worth seeking out.

Finally this chapter mentions natural accessories. These can make your flowers and foliage go further and add texture, colour and interest.

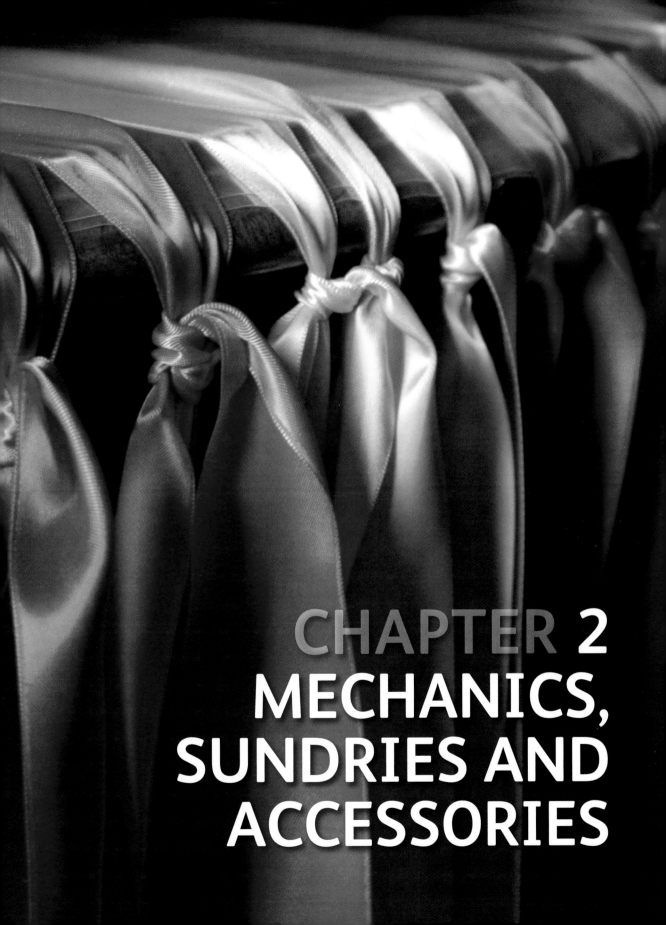

CHAPTER 2
MECHANICS, SUNDRIES AND ACCESSORIES

MECHANICS

Floral foam

Floral foam was invented in the 1940s by a chemist called Vernon Smithers. It is light and made of resins that restrict the growth of bacteria. Stems can be inserted at all angles, enabling designs to have graceful flow. One of the best-known foam brands world-wide is OASIS®. It can be purchased in different sizes and shapes – including cylinders, balls and cones – but most often in bricks. The green foam is used for arranging fresh plant material and there is a grey foam available designed for use with artificial flowers.

OASIS® Floral Foam Jumbo Bricks are a high-density version, which supports heavier stems with ease. These are purchased one (Jumbo 1 Brick) or three (Jumbo 3 Brick) to a box. The latter is the best as it is easier to handle. The single brick of foam needs a very large basin or a bath for soaking. With the addition of water it becomes very heavy and hard to lift. Jumbo Bricks eliminate the need to tape and wire several bricks together and are invaluable in pedestal and urn designs.

Soaking your foam

A brick of floral foam can absorb water to maximum capacity in under a minute. To soak foam correctly, fill a basin or bowl with water that is deeper and wider than the piece you wish to soak.

To prevent dry areas occurring (which will not provide water for the flowers), you should gently place the foam on the surface of the water. It will sink under its own weight until the foam is level with the water and the colour has changed from light to dark green. This will take approximately 60 seconds. Do not over-soak the foam or it will become spongy.

OASIS® Floral Foam Jumbo Bricks take longer to soak – perhaps ten times as long – but follow exactly the same method as for the brick.

Storing foam

If after use your foam is intact with only a few stem holes, you could keep it for future use. Place it in a plastic bag and tie firmly so that it is airtight, which will keep it moist. Once it has been wetted, the foam must not be allowed to dry out. If it does dry, add a drop of washing-up liquid to some boiling water and pour over the foam. You can then reuse it, but it will not retain water as efficiently.

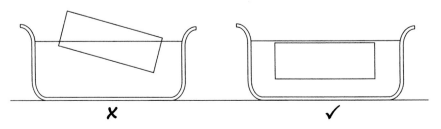

X   **✓**

right Using foam allows the arranger to angle stems gently over the rim of a container so the flowers and container are harmoniously one.

Pinholder

Pinholders come in many shapes and sizes. Only one pinholder is necessary for beginners. The most useful size is probably 6.25 cm (2½ in) in diameter, but 5 cm (2 in) or 7.5 cm (3 in) would be fine.

A good pinholder should have:

- brass (yellow) rather than steel (grey) pins because they do not rust
- a lead base that is heavy in the hand
- pins that are close together and firmly embedded in the lead
- a longer pin also is advantageous to give more possibilities of fixture.

If using a pinholder in conjunction with floral foam, first place a square of nylon cut from a pair of tights over the pins. It will otherwise be extremely difficult to remove all traces of the foam when dismantling your arrangement.

Cut hard stems at a sharp angle and then ease them between or on to the pins. Place in upright and then angle as desired using gentle pressure. If a stem refuses to stay in place, slit it upwards.

Thin stems are difficult to use on pinholders. Tie several together with wool and they will then slip easily on to a pin. Alternatively, place thin stems inside thicker hollow stems.

The pinholder can be placed on to a dish, but if you would prefer it to be more secure use florists' fix on the base (see page 53).

Flat pebbles, glass nuggets, moss or large leaves can be used to disguise the pinholder.

Chicken wire

Chicken wire is available in different mesh sizes and can be purchased from ironmongers, DIY stores and florists' wholesalers. The last of these stock green plastic-coated wire, which is more expensive but gentler on the hands and easier to manipulate.

Chicken wire can be used in the following ways:

Inside the container

This is the ideal method for securing soft stems and flowers that need lots of water, such as bulb flowers and hydrangeas. A good mesh size for this purpose is 5 cm (2 in) gauge. The amount you use depends on the size of the container and the thickness of the stems.

Follow these steps:

1 Cut a piece of chicken wire a little wider than the width of the container's opening and about three times the depth.

2 Remove the wire's selvedge as this is stiff and hard to manipulate.

3 Crumple the netting so that it follows the container's shape and wedge it firmly in the container.

4 Fill the container with water and thread your stems through the wire.

If your flowers need extra support, perhaps if you are using thick and heavy branches of blossom, place a pinholder in the bottom of your container. Ensure your first placement is firmly impaled on the pinholder, as this will secure the netting.

Around foam

When creating a large-scale arrangement, you will use heavy stems that may need extra support. A cap of small-gauge chicken wire placed gently over the foam and secured with wire around the container will give strength to your mechanics. Chicken wire with a 1.25 cm (½ in) gauge is suitable for this purpose. The larger 5 cm (2 in) chicken wire cuts into the foam too deeply.

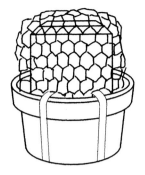

below Felix Geiling-Rasmus, a German Master Florist, created this design using hand-made chicken wire to create a structure on to which glass test tubes have been bound.

Aluminium wire

A small amount of lightly scrunched aluminium wire in a vase or basket is perfect for flowers that love water, such as bulb flowers.
The wire will give a certain amount of support to make arranging easier and will look attractive too.

Stems, sticks and twigs

A mesh of twigs is ideal for supporting stems or for hiding plastic or glass tubes containing water.

right Aluminium wire has been lightly scrunched in the hands to fit loosely inside the vase. It provides support for the daffodils which are far happier with their stems in water rather than foam.

Alternatively a grid can easily be created with straight woody stems, through which the stems can be slipped. Decorative wire or raffia-covered wire can be used to keep the grid in place.

right A bundle of birch twigs has been wound in the hands to create a nest. Once inside the glass cube the twigs provide a strong support for the soft-stemmed *Hyacinthoides hispanica* (Spanish bluebells) gently bound with raffia.

Glass and plastic tubes

Tubes made of glass or plastic are of great value to the flower designer. They support flowers neatly and decoratively and avoid the need for long stems (which can be expensive), as large plastic or metal tubes can be strapped to sticks to increase the height of the flowers in the design. A plastic tube can be disguised with a long-lasting leaf, such as ivy, secured with a blob of florists' fix, decorative wire or raffia.

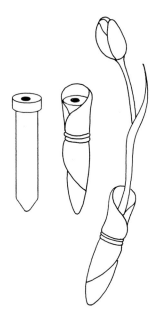

Aluminium wire can be wrapped around a glass tube, with the free end attached to a frame, branch or other support.

Transparent adhesive tape

Adheshive tape can quickly create a grid through which the stems can be placed. The plant material will hide the tape, which is easily disguised. Ensure that the bowl is dry and that you take the tape well over the sides. Once the arrangement has been made any ends that are visible can be removed. If the grid is large, I usually take a length of tape around the container, close to the rim, to make a stronger structure.

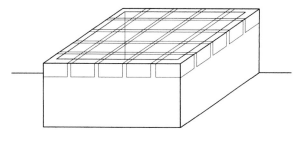

right A grid of clear adhesive tape provides support for a mixed tapestry of *Anemone*, berried *Hedera helix* 'Arborescens', *Viburnum opulus* and ming fern.

SUNDRIES

Scissors

I have started this section with scissors as they are probably the most important tool for a floral designer. They can be easily ordered online or purchased at your local garden centre.

Buying a good pair of floral scissors is essential. Household scissors will only frustrate you, squash the stems and cut your fingers. Your first pair of scissors should have medium-length blades and be specially designed for cutting flower stems. If there is a notch to facilitate cutting thick stems and wire it is a bonus, otherwise use special wire cutters available from DIY stores. They must also be easy to grasp. Check that there is enough room for your fingers and thumb to fit comfortably in the handles.

Florists' tape

This strong adhesive tape sticks firmly to both wet and dry foam. It is available in green, white and transparent. Wrap it around a container to keep the foam and container together as one. Avoid using too many widths across the foam, because this will limit the space for stems. Tape is readily available in two thicknesses. I prefer the wider tape as it gives better security. Pinch it across the top of the foam to make it narrower, thus taking up less space, leaving it wider down the sides.

When creating a symmetrical design, use the tape off-centre so you have the space to place a central stem.

Florists' fix

This is similar to Blu-Tack®, Plasticine® and chewing gum and you could use these as an alternative. Fix is used when two hard surfaces need to be held together securely but not permanently. It works most efficiently when the surfaces are dry and free of dust. For instance, a thin sausage of fix can be wrapped round the protruding knob of a candlecup to ensure it is secure in the candlestick.

Fix is difficult to remove, so if you are using a silver or brass candlestick protect it by taping transparent adhesive tape or clingfilm to the metal.

Fix is also used to secure foam holders (see below) and pinholders. It can be removed with turpentine or white spirit.

Foam holders

A foam holder (sometimes known as a 'frog') is a round plastic disc with four prongs. It can be used to secure foam to a container. Position a flat piece of fix on the dry underside of the frog. Fix the frog firmly in place in the container and put the foam on the prongs.

Plastic dishes and containers

The dishes illustrated will enable you to create a variety of designs. Do not worry if you cannot find them at your local garden centre – any small, shallow receptacle that retains water will work.

These dishes are useful, however, because they are:

- virtually unbreakable
- inexpensive, so if you are creating flowers for a large function there is no need for the containers to be collected
- easy to clean by hand or in a dishwater

Plastic tray with hanging handle

This inexpensive tray holds one third of a brick of foam. After taping the foam in place, suspend it by threading ribbon, wire or raffia through the hole in the handle. It can be used for wall arrangements or for hanging on pews and on the backs of chairs.

Floral rings

These are available in different diameters with either a plastic or a polystyrene base and the price varies only slightly. The plastic lip catches any drips and is therefore suitable for a table centrepiece. Leaves or ribbon can be pinned to the polystyrene base but would have to be glued to the plastic base.

Secateurs

These are invaluable for cutting strong and woody stems. Do not use to cut wires as they will quickly become blunt.

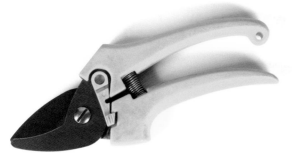

right *Gaultheria* (salal tips) and leatherleaf provide a backcloth to *Rosa* 'Avalanche', spray roses and spray *Chamelaucium* (waxflower)

Wires

Florists' wires are available in a wide range of lengths, weights (gauges) and colours. They support and lengthen stems and reduce weight by replacing the stems which are heavier. Coloured wires can also be decorative. The basic guideline is to use the lightest wire possible for your purpose. In the metric system the measurement dictates that the thicker the wire the higher the number. For those who are new to the art, I would suggest that you acquire three thicknesses of cut wire:

- heavy wires 1.00 mm or 1.25 mm
- medium wire of 0.90 mm
- light wire of 0.56 mm or 0.46 mm.

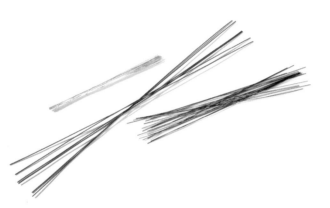

Also available:

- reel wire (binding wire) of 0.56 mm thickness suitable for mossing wreaths
- metallic, decorative reel wire in many colours, including copper, brass, gold, red and lime green to give attractive detail

- bullion is metallic wire but with a crinkly texture. It is available in different thicknesses and a range of colours. It also gives decorative detail
- mossing pins, rather like open hairpins, for pinning moss and leaves to foam

- coiled aluminium wire is available in different thicknesses, weights and colours. It can be used to give decorative details and to give support to stems in vases or baskets

- bindwire (paper-covered wire) is ideal for hanging arrangements where wire would slip or cause damage. It is also used for binding together branches and twigs securely. In addition, it can be made into a decorative feature.

Wire holders

These are extendable round plastic holders that keep your wires in place and are invaluable.

Stem tapes

Parafilm and Stemtex are the two best-known names for stem tapes. Parafilm is smooth and efficient and for me creates a neater, slimmer finish than Stemtex, which has a crêpey appearance and is slightly less expensive to purchase. Both stretch and adhere to the stem or wire if pulled tightly. They help to keep moisture in the stem and to give a more decorative finish. Stemtex is available in green, brown and white.

Stem cleaner

This is a relatively new invention by Smithers-OASIS®. Rather like a pet grooming pad, the stem cleaner is held in the hand and brought down the stem to remove leaves and thorns with ease. It is effective and inexpensive. Avoid complicated metal appliances which might also be effective but can damage the stems.

right This tall glass vase is filled with gel granules to which beads have been added. Aluminium wire covers orchid tubes, which are then linked to each other. Each tube contains the single head of the white *Phalaenopsis* orchid.

Candlecup

Candlesticks are often used for raised arrangements. To adapt them for flower arranging, all you need is a candlecup, which is a metal or plastic bowl with a protruding knob that inserts into the neck of the candlestick. They are widely available in white or black, but can be sprayed to match your container. If you cannot find a candlecup, glue a cork to the bottom of a small plastic dish.

To keep the candlecup from wobbling, you may need some florists' fix around the knob.

Candles

The range of candles available is immense. To anchor a slim taper candle in foam, use a specially designed holder. For thicker church-style candles, you will have to make do with a home-made version. Secure 5–7 short lengths of cocktail/kebab/garden stick on a piece of florists' tape, then wrap the tape tightly around the base of the candle. There should be only a small amount of stick above the tape. You could alternatively use stub wire bent into hairpins around the base of the candle, provided the candle is not too large. Do ensure that your candles are secure in the foam and never leave unattended when lit.

left and right Candles complete the picture and add mood and fragrance if so desired.

NATURAL ACCESSORIES

Moss

Moss gives texture, softness and colour to a design. The most commonly used mosses are:

- **_Sphagnum_ moss**
  This retains moisture and is ideal for wreaths and hanging baskets. It is used for these properties rather than for its colour, which tends to be on the straw side of green.

- **_Plagiothecium undulatum_ (carpet/flat moss)**
  This is a strong green and has a flat earth backing. It is perfect for covering large areas quickly and evenly.

- **_Cladonia rangiferina_ (reindeer moss)**
  A soft, spongy moss that has been treated with a softening agent, such as glycerine, to which a dye is often added. Natural and green-coloured reindeer moss is recommended for giving wonderful texture and for hiding mechanics.

- **_Leucobryum glaucum_ (bun moss)**
  Available in gently undulating green mounds.

- **_Tillandsia usneoides_ (Spanish moss)**
  The natural grey hanging strands of these air plants are excellent for covering surfaces and adding texture.

left to right
Sphagnum moss, _Plagiothecium undulatum_ (carpet/flat moss), _Tillandsia usneoides_ (Spanish moss), _Leucobryum glaucum_ (bun moss).

Stones and pebbles (aggregates)

The smooth form and texture of stones and pebbles make them ideal for incorporating in arrangements. Coloured gravel adds interest to designs.

left to right
coloured glass nuggets, aggregates, large grey pebbles, shells.

To revive carpet/flat moss that is losing its colour,
pour very hot water over the moss. This seems to
work only once.

Raffia

Raffia provides a natural tie that enhances rather than detracts from the flowers. Neutral and green raffia always work well.

Sisal

Sisal is produced from the leaves of *Agave sisalana* and is dyed many colours. It gives excellent texture and easy cover. It can be secured to foam with wire or German pins.

Cones

Cones of all sizes and from all conifers are useful to flower designers.

To mount small to medium-sized cones, wrap a wire around the lowest part of the cone, between the scales, pulling it tight but leaving each end loose. Take the loose ends, bring them together under the base of the cone and twist to form your stalk.

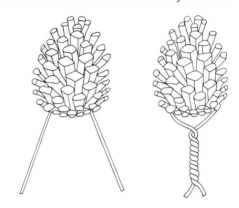

Use two wires to mount larger cones. Hold both wires horizontally, one on either side of the cone, and force each of them as low as possible between the scales. Twist the two ends on either side together. Pull under the base of the cone and twist together to form a stalk.

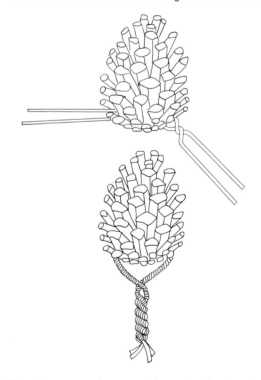

Closed cones can have a stick or wire glued to their base. Cones easily take spray paint to give colour and interest in a design.

below Cones on wire supports add interest and festive cheer to this ring of roses on a conifer base.

Sticks and canes

The following are widely used in design work:

Giunno
Short pre-cut sticks bagged in assorted lengths in
different colour tones.

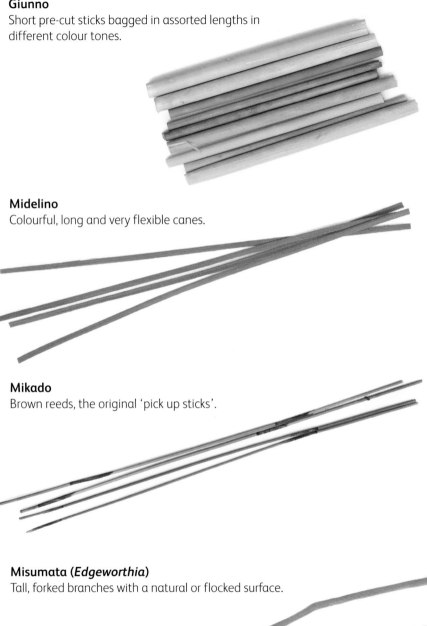

Midelino
Colourful, long and very flexible canes.

Mikado
Brown reeds, the original 'pick up sticks'.

Misumata (*Edgeworthia*)
Tall, forked branches with a natural or flocked surface.

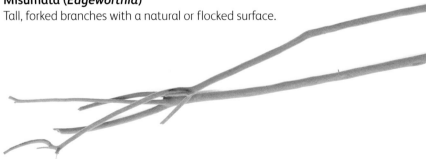

left Cut lengths of midelino create impact and strong design in an arrangement of *Freesia*, waxflower and *Rosa* 'Ocean Song'.

Fruit and vegetables

Fruit and vegetables add interest and give form, colour and texture. In practical terms fruit and vegetables should not be placed near flowers since the ethylene gas given off as they ripen accelerates the flowers' ageing process. Do take this into account if you want your plant material to last as long as possible.

To give the fruit and vegetables a 'stalk' you could use either of the methods below:

Take a medium- or heavy-gauge wire through the fruit and out the far side, about one-third of the way up the fruit. Repeat with a second wire at right-angles to the first. Bring the wires down and twist together.

Insert wooden or plastic sticks into the fruit. This 'stalk' is not flexible but the method is ideal for small items as it is quick and easy and the fruit can be eaten afterwards.

right An inexpensive autumnal centrepiece has been created with sprigs of berried *Hedera helix* 'Arborescens' (tree ivy) and *Hydrangea* with the wired green apples substituting for round flowers and the grapes for spray!

I thoroughly enjoyed creating these designs using flowering rhubarb and leeks from my local greengrocer.

left What could be simpler! Stems of beautiful, flowering rhubarb have been placed in a tumbler of water. A tie of raffia keeps the stems in place. Ten stems of blue *Anemone* rest with their heads on the rim of the glass tumbler.

right A wrap of double-sided tape is taken round the centre of a glass tumbler. Leeks are pressed on to the tape and raffia bound round the stems to give security. Stems of rose hips are inserted between the stems of the leeks. Double sided tape is again used on two small jam jars on to which autumnal leaves have been pressed. A few spray roses in the same colour as the hips complete the design.

*F*orm, texture, colour and space are the **elements** of design. When selecting your flowers and foliage to create an arrangement, you should always be aware of the simple guidelines that relate to these elements to ease your choice.

After selecting your flowers, there are certain **principles** that will ensure your work is pleasing to the eye. They are balance, scale, proportion, rhythm, contrast and dominance.

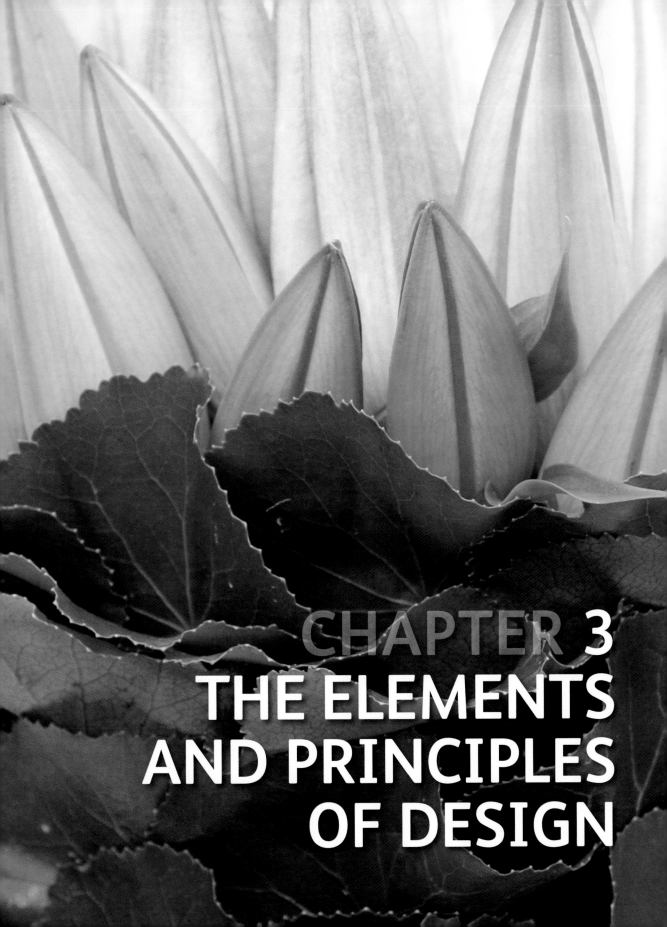

CHAPTER 3
THE ELEMENTS AND PRINCIPLES OF DESIGN

THE ELEMENTS OF DESIGN

Form

Form describes the three-dimensional, volumetric 'shape' of a flower or foliage stem. 'Shape' is normally used to describe something two-dimensional or flat – such as writing on a page.

The form of flowers and foliage can be categorised loosely as:

- round
- spray
- line

The flower A–Z in Chapter 1 shows the categories in which a wide range of plant material belong.

Round

Round, circular forms are the focus of any arrangement. They are the stars of the design because the eye is automatically drawn to them. You therefore need at least one round flower in a design of mixed blooms to hold and focus the eye.

Dianthus (carnation)   *Gerbera*

There are many round flowers to choose from, such as carnations, bloom chrysanthemums, *Dahlia*, *Hydrangea*, open lilies, *Paeonia* (peony), open roses and sunflowers. I have also grouped the heart-shaped *Anthurium* under this heading in Chapter 1.

Spray

Spray flowers and berries offer softness and contrast. In a design of mixed flowers, they are the supporting acts to the more dominant round form. Examples include *Alchemilla mollis* (lady's mantle), *Bupleurum*, *Euphorbia*, *Gypsophila*, *Hypericum* and *Solidago* (golden rod).

Alchemilla mollis (lady's mantle)

Line

Line flowers such as *Aconitum* (monkshood), *Delphinium* and *Gladiolus* are used in large designs to bring colour and texture from the edges into the centre. They are also used extensively in parallel designs and in contemporary work.

Delphinium

right This arrangement shows the value of the three different forms when combined together. *Eremurus* give line, *Helianthus* (sunflower) provides round and *Alstroemeria* spray. On their own a mass of any of these three flowers would give good design, but when combined the round form holds the eye and provides harmony with the other forms.

Texture

Texture refers to how we imagine a flower or leaf will feel when touched. An arrangement's interest is intensified through the use of a variety of contrasting textures.

Think of a teasel. How do you imagine it would feel to touch? Prickly is the word we use to describe its texture. *Stachys* leaves can be termed felted and *Alchemilla mollis* soft.

Smooth texture

It is important to include a minimum of one foliage or flower with a smooth texture in arrangements of mixed blooms, because it will hold together all the other elements. Smooth leaves include *Aspidistra*, *Eucalyptus*, *Hedera* (ivy), *Hosta* and *Parthenocissus tricuspidata* (Boston ivy). Round, many-petalled composite flowers such as *Chrysanthemum* and *Gerbera* are smooth, as are many seedheads, berries, fruit and vegetables.

right The material of the container has a bearing on the volume of flowers easily sustained. A heavy ceramic or stone container will support a greater volume of flowers than one of glass or porcelain. Here my favourite container holds fragrant stocks, glorious blue summer *Scabiosa*, roses, *Leucadendron* 'Safari Sunset' and green blackberries. The slate table adds weight at the base of the design.

The crab apples have a smooth texture, the conifer rough and the grey Stachys lanata leaves feel like velvet!

Arrangements where texture is of extra importance

Good textural contrasts are important in arrangements when the:

- colour scheme is monochromatic
- light is poor
- plant material is dried not fresh
- height of the plant material is relatively level, such as in tapestry work
- colour scheme is composed of pale colours rather than a mix of bold

left In this design of pastels the textural contrast between the smooth roses and the multi-faceted *Hydrangea* is important for good design.

below In this intricate embroidered tapestry the use of smooth-textured berries, roses and *Galax* against the more intricate plant material gives contrast of texture and enables appreciation of all aspects of the design.

Using a limited range of plant material, this wreath of pepper berries and Eucalyptus relies on strong textural contrasts for impact.

Colour

Colour is perhaps the most emotive and important aspect of any design. The endless permutations and combinations never cease to amaze and excite.

Entire books have been written about colour, and they are of immense value to those wanting to study the subject in depth. Here are guidelines to help you use colour effectively.

Link colours by using green

In flower arranging, green is a 'neutral' colour. Whatever flowers you choose – for example, red roses with yellow *Alstroemeria* and orange *Gerbera* – the combination will work if you add lots of plain green foliage.

Lime green adds vitality

Lime-green flowers such as *Alchemilla mollis*, spray *Chrysanthemum* 'Kermit', *Chrysanthemum* 'Anastasia' and *Moluccella laevis* (bells of Ireland) will give zing and harmonise with all the other colours of the rainbow.

left *Viburnum opulus* (guelder rose) is much loved by flower arrangers and florists. Its lime-green colour adds freshness to any spring combination of flowers. Here it is combined with purple and white *Syringa*.

right *Alchemilla mollis* is another lime-green plant, easy to grow in the garden in a damp and shady spot. It is invaluable in design through the summer and early autumn.

Add light to dark and dark to light

If your arrangement is predominantly composed of pale colours, introduce some dark flowers or foliage, such as dark burgundy *Leucadendron* 'Safari Sunset' or *Heuchera* leaves to give depth and heighten interest. Conversely, if the arrangement is of dark, subdued colours, introduce a lighter tint, such as cream spray roses, to give vitality.

Link flowers to the seasons

Colours are linked to the seasons, both in the mind and in what is seasonally available. Traditionally we think of blue, yellow and pink in spring, mixed colours in summer, strong deep tones of yellow, orange, burgundy and terracotta for autumn and red, green, white and gold during the winter months.

Colours for large and small areas – advancing and receding colours

Colour needs to be considered when arranging flowers in a large setting. Blues and violets, known as receding colours, disappear when viewed from a distance or in poor light. Conversely, warm colours such as yellow, orange and red advance and can be seen much more clearly. They can be used to great effect in a room that you want to appear more intimate. The more white in a colour, the more visible it will be. For example, lemon is more visible than gold and pink is more visible than burgundy.

In candlelight pastel colours (tints) show up best, where receding colours such as blues and violets will disappear.

advancing colours   receding colours

Colours for special occasions

For Valentine's Day we think of red, for Halloween purple, orange and black and for Christmas gold, red, white and green. Silver would be chosen for a 25th wedding anniversary and pinks for a baby girl's christening. Often white or cream is chosen for a traditional wedding.

Link the colour with the container

Link the colour of the flowers with that of the container. Copper and brass vases encourage the use of red, bronze and peach plant material. Aluminium and cream containers work well with white, cream and pink flowers.

above Grey containers work well with all flower colours but are particularly effective with pink or cream.

Warm and cool colours

Reds, orange and gold yellows are warm colours and work happily together. Blues, purples and sharp yellows are cool colours and are harmonious in the same design.

White

Although white is not a true colour is it much loved by British designers. White flowers are very visible and are best presented in white or neutral containers (such as grey) which do not compete with the strength of their visibility.

right The white roses, stocks and *Eustoma* work harmoniously with the container. Depth and interest are added with the inclusion of a few sprays of burgundy *Berberis*.

Colour combinations

The colour wheel is fascinating. It uses three principal (primary) colours – red, blue and yellow. These are the only colours that cannot be obtained by mixing two or more colours together. These principal colours can be mixed to provide further colours. A straight mix of red and blue provides purple; blue and yellow produce green; and yellow and red make orange. Purple, green and orange are termed secondary colours. Green is considered a neutral colour and can be added to any colour scheme.

Tints

Tints are acquired by adding white to the primary and secondary colours. For example, a tint of red is pink, a tint of yellow is lemon. A synonym for tint is pastel.

Shades

Shades are acquired by adding black. A shade of red is maroon and a shade of blue is navy.

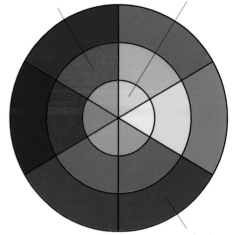

'pure' primary or secondary colours

tints or pastels – where white has been added

shades – where black has been added

above The colour wheel

Colour schemes

Monochromatic colour scheme

A monochromatic colour scheme can use tints, shades and the full intensity of a single colour. Interest in the arrangement can be heightened by the use of strong textural contrasts. This is an easy colour scheme to use.

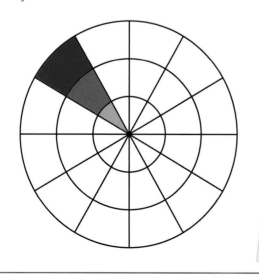

Flowers in varying tints and shades of blue illustrate a monochromatic colour palette

right Winter-flowering blue *Anemone* have been combined with the blue-black heads of *Hedera helix* 'Arborescens' (fruiting tree ivy) to create a monochromatic colour scheme with neutral green.

Adjacent colour scheme

An adjacent colour scheme uses up to one-third of a colour wheel, the colours all being found next to each other. In flower arranging it is accepted that green may also be included. One example would be green-yellow, yellow, yellow-orange and orange, plus green. This colour scheme is also a safe option.

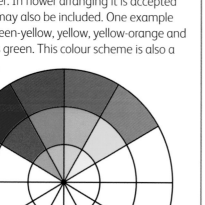

right *Helleborus* leaves and *Skimmia japonica* create the background to this arrangement of flowers using the adjacent colour scheme of red *Celosia*, *Hypericum* and roses with orange spray roses.

Orange through red to pink illustrates a harmonious combination of adjacent colours.

Complementary colour scheme

A more dynamic colour scheme is achieved by combining colours from opposite sides of the wheel such as yellow and purple. Any two complementary colours used together will intensify and enhance each other brilliantly. Put blue flowers against an orange background and observe their clarity. Avoid using equal amounts of the two colours. Conversely, do not use just one flower of a different colour as it will be too dominant.

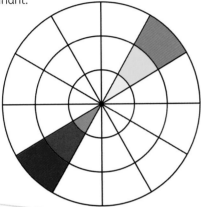

Polychromatic colour scheme

This is the use of many colours together. A polychromatic colour scheme is always cheerful and vibrant. The use of plain green foliage brings all the colours together harmoniously.

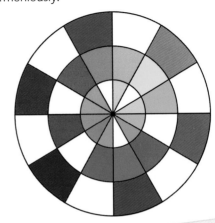

The vibrant yellow tulips contrast strikingly with the purple hyacinths.

In nature, flowers from all aspects of the colour wheel live happily side by side – they are united by green foliage.

below A casually arranged
line of eclectic containers
holding flowers of every
colour of the spectrum.

below I love this design by Lana Bates showing the power of enclosed space. The space balances the plant material on the left of the design, which occupies only slightly more space within the circle.

Space

Solid is the opposite of space; without space there is no form. The Japanese art of Ikebana makes good use of space and it is to this ancient art that many Western designers turn for inspiration. Space emphasises form. If, for example, there is space around a *Gerbera* you can see its form clearly. Space can be incorporated into a flower arrangement in the following ways.

Within the arrangement

Classic design incorporates more space at the limits of the design than at the focal area. The use of space allows different planes and angles to be incorporated, thus increasing overall interest in the design.

In a contemporary design of limited material, space can be used to balance form, colour and texture. Space can have as much eye-pull as a solid form, particularly when enclosed by manipulation of leaves or loops of cane, raffia or plant material.

In massed contemporary designs – such as a tapestry/pavé – there is little space within. However, space can be incorporated by placing plant material at varying levels using bridge material such as driftwood or flexible grasses or by simply using volumetric flower forms with space within.

left The fresh *Cornus* (dogwood) stems are flexible and easily manipulated into loops to create space within the design.

Underneath the container

With urns and footed containers the space around the stem of the container is also an important part of the design.

In the setting

It is vital to position your arrangement so that it is surrounded by space. Here, space is allied to proportion and scale. Perhaps the easiest way to grasp this point is to imagine a niche. The arrangement should fill approximately two-thirds of the space and no more. Conversely, the arrangement should not be so small in proportion to its surroundings that it becomes insignificant.

Inside the container

Contemporary design often features flowers within the container, but the relationship of flowers to space should be in the proportion of 1½:1 or vice versa.

right A round glass bowl holds a small amount of fresh water. Flexible *Ornithogalum* (chincherinchee) have been gently wound around the inside of the bowl to give a design of interwoven stems and gently flowering blooms. The space within the bowl allows the design of stems and flowering blooms to be fully appreciated.

THE PRINCIPLES OF DESIGN

Balance

A flower arrangement should have physical (actual) and visual balance. Good balance is considered not simply from side to side but also from top to bottom and front to back.

Physical balance

Physical balance means that the arrangement will not topple over. To prevent this happening, the container or vase must be large enough for the number of flowers being used and the mechanics must be sound and secure. Ensure that the flowers are evenly distributed in the arrangement, with plant material at the back so that it does not fall forward.

Visual balance

If your arrangement is unlikely to fall over but looks as if it might, the visual balance needs adjusting. The arrangement will be pleasing to the eye only if there is stability in the design and it does not make you feel anxious.

Types of balance

Symmetrical balance

True symmetrical balance is achieved when one side of an arrangement is identical to the other. Flower arranging is, however, less contrived and the term 'symmetrical balance' is used when both sides are more or less equal in terms of visual weight.

Symmetrical arrangements are used in settings where the areas exposed on both sides are similar – such as on the centre of a table or the centre of a mantelpiece.

Asymmetrical balance

Asymmetrical balance is harder to understand and achieve. The visual weight of the plant material is different on each side of the central axis. Although the elements are different, balance is usually achieved by placement. Usually, such a design is placed to one side of a desk, table or mantelpiece, and is balanced by an object such as a lamp on the other side.

Key points for achieving good balance

- Rounded forms usually appear heavier than linear forms.
- Visual weight increases:
  - the further the materials are from the central axis
  - the stronger they are in colour
  - the warmer they are in hue
  - the larger the form.
- Colours that advance, such as yellows and oranges, have more visual strength than colours that recede, such as blues and purples.
- Shiny textures have more dominance than dull textures.

Good balance means the arrangement is not just balanced visually in terms of weight from side to side but also from top to bottom and front to back.

left In this design by Stef Adriaenssens, the asymmetric use of balance is one of the finest examples I have ever seen. Here the movement of the container perfectly balances the glued coils of flat cane that are attached to the wired central axis. The judicious plucked stems of soft ruscus and the careful placement of the tiny daisy flowers in glass tubes complete a design that fills me with joy.

Proportion

Proportion is the word that is used to describe one part of your arrangement in relation to the other parts and to the arrangement as a whole.

The foundations for good proportion were laid down by the ancient Greeks. Their discoveries, sometimes called the *golden section* or the *golden mean*, have stood the test of time and give pleasing results. AC is to AB as CB is to AC. This theory also applies to areas and volumes. An easy-to-remember summary is that the ideal proportions of one part to another is 1.68:1 but for simplification this is adjusted to 1.5:1. This is the basis for the guidelines to good proportion shown in this book given in terms of 1½:1.

Applied to flower arranging, the *golden mean* can be broadly summed up by considering either volume (a mass of plant material) or height (when relatively few stems are involved). This is not as difficult as it sounds.

Volume

If you have a mass of plant material – such as when arranging flowers in a vase – consider the relationship in volume between the plant material and the container. Either the flowers or the container should dominate and the relationship between the two parts should be 1½:1. There should never be equal eye-pull demanded by both parts, however harmonious it might be in terms of colour, form and texture.

A   **C**   **B**

AC is to AB as CB is to AC

An abundance of Daucus carota (Queen Anne's lace) has good proportions in relation to the vase.

left Good classic proportions of flowers to container. The *Syringa* (lilac), *Viburnum opulus*, *Ranunculus* and tulips dominate but do not overwhelm the textured vase.

Height and width

If you have only relatively few stems think in terms of height.

- If your container is low, the tallest stem should be one and a half times (or a little more) the width of the container.
- If the container is tall and the movement flowing upwards, the height should be about one and a half times the height of the container.

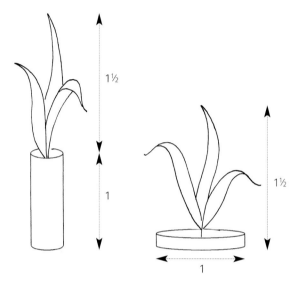

Positioning of flowers

You should also consider whether your flowers are in proportion to their setting. Very simply, this means that for a large reception you would not use a thimble containing wild flowers. Proportion is closely linked with scale.

left There are exceptions to every rule, I am glad to say. Here the mass of flowers to vase is pretty equal but the lime of the *Viburnum opulus* links so well with the green of the container that the rule is overruled!

right Where the movement of the plant material is visually upwards the height should relate to that of the container in the proportions of 1½:1.

left Contemporary proportions with the volume of the vase dominating the flowers in the approximate proportion of 1½ :1.

right Tulips, tumbling out of a tulipière, are positioned on a bare window ledge with plenty of space around to show off their beauty.

Rhythm

Rhythm is the hardest of the principles to explain. It is best understood by using words from music such as movement and beat. In an arrangement with good rhythm, the eye moves through the arrangement by the following means.

Repetition

Repetition, such as a row of five similar vases on a table, leads the eye along. Repetition of colours, forms, textures and space takes the eye through the design – the eye instinctively looks for association.

above Circular rhythm.

right Vertical rhythm.

above Horizontal rhythm.

right Rhythm through
repetition of the loops of
Salix (willow). Rhythm also
exists through the repetition
of the form of the *Eustoma*
(lisianthus) with the pattern
on the container.

Radiating lines

Radiation is one of the most pleasing means of creating good rhythm. Lines that flow uninterrupted from a central point give a feeling of movement. This feeling is dispelled if any of the lines cross, so interrupting the rhythm.

Transition

In classic design the graduation of size, form and colour gently leads the eye in and out of the arrangement.

left In this classic flowers in a vase design, the flowers gently radiate from the centre of the vase. The addition of the *Salix* (pussy willow) adds additional movement.

right The sinuous intertwining curves of the *Zantedeschia* stems add movement to this design of roses, *Hydrangea* and hanging *Amaranthus*.

Contrast

Contrast is the difference shown when objects are placed next to each other. When using different forms and textures, the contrast can be obvious, but there is also subtle contrast when a mass of flowers of the same variety are placed in a vase. The contrast is then based on the different length of the stems and the flowers in their various states of development and the contrast between the plant material and the container.

Contrast of form

When using more than one type of plant material, avoid arranging similar materials that do not have sufficient contrast. Always use at least one flower with a round form.

Contrast of colour

Complementary colours make the strongest contrast. If the colours have gentle contrast, strong contrasts of form and texture are often required.

Contrast of texture

Strong textural contrasts are often needed in monochromatic designs.

below Contrast of colour, form and texture with David Austin roses, mother-of-pearl shells, lotus seedheads, *Viburnum tinus* berries and *Diplocyclos palmatus* (lollipop climber).

Dominance

If a flower design contains two or more equal attractions, they will pull the design apart. Without dominance, there is lack of unity and harmony. Dominance provides a sense of order. Dominance is often linked to proportion.

There should always be:

- Dominant texture. A smooth shiny texture is more compelling than a rough texture. Always allow one texture to dominate.

- Dominant movement. This can be vertical, horizontal, circular or angular.

- Dominant form. One form should dominate but there should also be other forms for good visual proportion. Round is the most dominant form by virtue of eye attraction and weight.

- Dominant colour. Pale colours are more dominant than darker ones. Therefore if you use a combination of light and dark, ensure that these are also in proportion.

right The roses in this design dominate by virtue of their colour, form and texture against the thyme and dried leaves on a bed of small stones.

below This bold and striking design of massed *Phalaenopsis* orchids, roses and *Chrysanthemum* 'Kermit' worked well in the large atrium at Chicheley Hall.

Scale

Scale is the relationship between each element of the design – each individual piece of plant material.

- It is important to consider the size of each flower and stem of foliage in relation to others. A *Hydrangea* would not rest comfortably with a daisy. *Convallaria* (lily-of-the-valley) would be dwarfed by a *Gerbera*. My guideline is that no flower should be more than twice the size of the one placed next to it (except if in a contemporary design).

- The size of the container and your plant material should be in scale – in terms of both size and texture.

- Think of the setting in which your arrangement will be displayed. A large hall has need of a large arrangement with bold plant material. The rooms of a small flat would be in scale with an arrangement of smaller flowers and foliage.

left *Muscari* are delicate spring blooms and here are combined with small-scale *Taxus baccata* (yew), *Hebe* and *Pittosporum* garden foliage and spray roses.

𝒯o get started all you need is an inexpensive vase available from home stores or supermarkets. This chapter explains how flowers can be effectively arranged in such a vase easily and without great expense. It also describes the technique for a handtied bouquet which looks beautiful in a clean glass vase. Its spiralled stems are an important part of the design.

CHAPTER 4
FLOWERS IN A VASE
AND HANDTIEDS

FLOWERS IN A VASE

Choosing the plant material

If you follow the guidelines below, your designs will always look successful.

- When mixing your flowers, always include at least one variety that has a round form, such as *Gerbera*, *Hydrangea* or open roses.

- When using a mass of flowers and foliage for a classic design, the volume of the plant material should be one and a half times the volume of the container. Alternatively, in contemporary design, the container can be one and a half times the volume of the flowers. The flowers and the vase should not be of equal volume. One needs to dominate to give visual harmony.

- A mass of one variety of flower is always attractive. You can arrange one variety together in different hues – from one end of the colour spectrum to the other. They will always look good if the container and flowers are in proportion.

right A mass of *Anemone*, in hues of pink and blue, are arranged in water in the pleasing proportions of 1½:1.

left *Alstroemeria*, *Celosia* and roses – three different flowers in three different containers but linked by the use of tints and shades of the colour red.

- Add plain green (rather than variegated) foliage to a mixed bouquet of flowers. It will act as a harmoniser of all the other elements in the design, whatever the colour combination. If the flowers are pastels adding dark foliage can be effective.

- If you have only a few flowers, do not think of volume in relation to the container, but height. It should be one and a half to twice the height of the container to compensate for the lack of mass.

right With a few flowers good proportion is achieved by using stems that are twice the height of the container – in this example two callas are combined with *Salix* (golden willow) stems.

left Colour harmony is one of the most important elements of design. Here the combination of red *Cordyline* and *Gaultheria* (salal tips) are woven into a mix of rough textured *Sedum* and rich velvety roses.

- Reflect the colour of your vase in the flowers used. Copper is good with pinks, peaches, mauves, apricots and reds. Brass suits creams, yellows, oranges, greens and browns. Silver, alabaster and pewter are lovely with cream, white, pink, blue and grey.

below A tea cup may not seem the obvious choice for a vase but for small-scale garden snippets the arrangement is delightful, especially when linked to the colour and style of the china.

right The translucency of glass shows off the clean smooth stems of the tulips. *Kerria japonica*, which flowers so freely in the spring, gives delicacy and volume to the arrangement.

- Try grouping a mixture of containers together and then adding just one variety of flower in each. The containers can be different or have a common theme such as the colour white.

- Bear, steel and flexi grasses, or foliage with a natural bend such as *Eucalyptus* give movement and interest to designs in a vase.

above Three containers, each holding different flowers – *Galanthus* (snowdrops), *Helleborus* and *Viburnum opulus* (snowball tree). The green and white colours provide the harmonising link.

right One variety of flower (*Anemone*) in gentle tints and tones links the use of disparate white containers to give a pleasing whole.

Choosing a vase

If you are overwhelmed by the range and diversity of vases on offer, you would be safe to select:

- two or three straight-sided glass vases of various sizes. One could be a 15 cm (6 in) cube and the others smaller or larger depending on your home.

- a plain, sculptural vase in a classic, undemanding colour and texture.

The most useful height for a vase is 20 cm (8 in). This is probably shorter than you would have thought, but it is perfect for many flowers.

right The same 10 tulips arranged in a variety of vases to show the different effect the containers can create.

top A selection of contemporary containers.

below Classic-inspired containers.

Before you start

Make sure that your vase is sparkling clean. This is imperative both aesthetically and to protect the flowers. To remove lime-scale, use a product such as Viakal. To remove smears, use a proprietary window cleaner and a clean cloth. Make sure that there are no traces of either product left to contaminate the water. Do this by sterilising the vase with a product such as Milton, which will remove all bacteria.

Classic flowers in a vase

For classic design, at the risk of repetition, it is so important that the volume of flowers to container of approximately 1½:1.

In order to achieve this I recommend that the length of the first stem you place is twice as high as the vase. Once inside the vase it will be the height of the vase above the rim. Creating a grid of adhesive tape will hold this initial stem in place as you insert others. As a guide, further stems should be approximately the same length.

For the ideal bouquet aim to angle stems of plant material over the rim of the container. This will create perfect proportions. Also, if the rim is left exposed your flowers may appear to emerge uncomfortably from the vase and to sit on the vase rather than being in harmony.

Use a mass of seasonal flowers if they are available, otherwise start with foliage from the garden or florist – perhaps *Ligustrum* (privet), *Ribes sanguineum* (flowering currant), *Hebe* or *Gaultheria* (salal tips), hard ruscus or *Eucalyptus*.

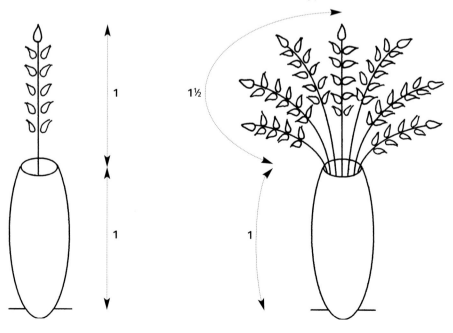

right In this design I had the joy of working with 50 parrot tulips. For the size of the container a mix of foliage with 15 tulips would also have worked well. With one type of flower use several different foliages (including variegated varieties). With a variety of flowers keep to one or two foliages – any more and it could get fussy. Here three *Fatsia* leaves are shown in the vase for decoration.

left A short tank vase works with the towering stems of *Hippeastrum* (amaryllis) three times its height. Why? Primarily, because there are no sharp contrasts. The *Salix* (willow) stems, within the glass container, lead the eye vertically upwards along the smooth stems to the limited number of flowers without disturbance. Every rule is meant to be broken!

Contemporary flowers in a vase

Try inserting one container into another. The inner one, which will not be seen, could be a mug or glass.
Fill the space between with plant material of your choice, such as lengths of pussy willow, coffee beans, cinnamon sticks or even jelly beans. Arrange your flowers in water or foam placed in the inner container.

If you are using foliage that will last well under water you can simply immerse it and use it as a mechanic to position your flowers.

left Take three long-lasting flower heads and wire them together with a length of reel wire, which is also attached to a glass balloon weight (from balloon specialists). Immerse under water in a tall container. Place the container inside a ring container holding votives and floating rose heads.

left There are many ways of presenting flowers within the vase which are pleasing. Flowers love to have short stems with direct access to water. Here white roses pack the base of the cylindrical vase, while a swirl of flexi grass gives definition to the space above.

below Flowers with naturally flexible stems are ideal for the inside of a fish bowl. Think *Zantedeschia* (calla), tulips and *Ornithogalum*. Leave them out of water for 30 minutes so they are flexible, recut the stems and place in shallow water within the fish bowl so that the ends are in water. Add a few beautiful shells, beads or wire of choice. Here *Zantedeschia* are wound around the bowl with strands of *Liriope* (lily grass) with shells of one type lying at the base.

HANDTIEDS

A handtied is a bunch of flowers arranged in the hand so that the stems create a spiral that is part of the design. It is the perfect gift, as the recipient needs only remove the wrapping, cut the twine and place in a vase. Aquapack wrapping – where the flowers are presented in water – means that they do not even have to cut the stems. A glass vase is ideal for a handtied so that the spiral of stems can be seen and appreciated.

Once you have mastered the spiralling technique, you will find that creating handtieds is highly relaxing. Most people need a few attempts to get the knack of creating the spiral, but then they never look back.

What to choose

✓ At least one variety of flower with a round form, such as mini *Gerbera*, peonies, roses or sunflowers.
✓ Spray flowers that branch high up the stem, as they add interest to the bouquet and give contrast to the round forms.
✓ Flowers with approximately the same life span.
✓ Flowers with strong stems, such as roses.
✓ Long-lasting foliage, such as *Ligustrum* (privet), *Gaultheria* (salal tips), rosemary or hard ruscus.
✓ Rough-textured twine for tying.

What not to choose

✗ Flowers that are in tight bud, because you will want immediate impact.
✗ Flowers with soft stems (such as daffodils and anemones), because they may be squashed when tied.
✗ Spray flowers that branch low down, such as spray carnations or *Eustoma* (lisianthus), because the lower flowers will need to be removed.
✗ Smooth, round, thick stems – these tend to slip as you cross one over the other.
✗ Smooth-textured string, as this will slip on the stems and not give a firm tie.

Tie the spiralled stems with a rough-textured twine or florists' bindwire. Anything that is smooth-textured will slip on the stems.

right A spiralled handtied of *Eucalyptus*, roses, tulips and bloom *Chrysanthemum*. Note that the softer-stemmed tulips have been placed within the design with a strong foliage surround so that the tie does not break any soft stems.

above A grouped handtied around
one beautiful blue *Hydrangea*. The
groups are created from *Eustoma*
(lisianthus), *Rosa* 'Cool Water' and
Limonium (statice) (centre). The whole
is surrounded by trails of green
hanging *Amaranthus*.

right This glorious handtied of *Eucalyptus*, *Dianthus*
(carnations), *Freesia*, lilies and berries by the German
Master Florist Felix Geiling-Rasmus would be difficult to
re-create. He breaks all the rules and makes the flowers
work for him effortlessly! Movement has been created by
the inclusion of the distinctive white stems of stripped
olive branches.

Classic spiral handtied

A classic handtied takes a mix of flowers and foliage and works them together so that the spiralled stems are an integral part of the design. Here we take a mix of flowers and create the perfect handtied.

Tip

For those of you who approach making a handtied with trepidation I suggest replacing the soft bulb flowers (hyacinths and tulips) – as shown in the handtied on page 139 – for flowers with stronger stems. The woodier the stems the less likely they are to break.

You will need

- **7–9 round flowers**
- **5–7 spray flowers**
- **a few stems of a third flower (spray or round) of choice**
- **foliage – half a bunch of *Gaultheria* (salal tips), stems of *Ligustrum* (privet) or a mix of foliage, as shown on page 139, of *Hedera helix* (ivy) and *Asparagus* fern.**

Method

1 Cut a length of garden twine about 50 cm (20 in) long. Place this around your neck so you know exactly where it is when it comes to tying the bouquet.

2 Remove all leaves from the lower two-thirds of each stem. All exposed stems must be immaculately clean so as to keep the water clear when displayed. Thorns should be carefully removed from roses.

3 Place your flowers and foliage in groups on a clean, uncluttered surface.

4 Bend your left arm (if right-handed) or right arm (if left-handed) so that the palm of your hand is facing you with the thumb uppermost. Close the fingers firmly, leaving the thumb flexible so that stems can be placed between the thumb and the palm of the hand.

5 To create a spiral of stems, angle them in the same direction around a central pivot.

a) Insert a central vertical stem between the palm of your hand and your thumb.

b) Angle a second stem across the first, with the head of the flower pointing towards the shoulder of the hand holding the flowers. This stem must cross the first stem cleanly and obviously. It should not lie parallel with the first stem.

c) Place a third stem at a sharper angle to the second stem so that the bouquet becomes wider at both the top and the bottom in different directions, creating a fan shape above the hand and below. Repeat this action with further stems.

d) As you create your handtied you may be concerned that the distribution of flowers is not perfect and therefore it is not balanced. This can be corrected by adding flowers to the rear of the design. To do this, relax your hand and tuck the next stem between the stems you have now spiralled and the palm of your hand so that the head of the flower now points towards the shoulder of the hand adding (not holding) the flowers. By doing this, the flowers will circle round in the same direction.

e) Continue building up the spiral by adding more stems to the first direction and behind when you need to balance the material.

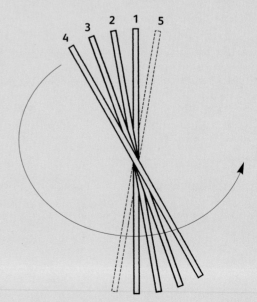

Note: you may become concerned that your bouquet is flat rather than rounded. With a little experience, you will be able to relax your hand and achieve a more rounded form to the handtied.

f) When all your stems have been included, wrap them with garden twine round the point where they cross over (above your hand not below). Tie as high as you can on the bare stems with a knot or bow. Avoid tying over any leaves.

g) Cut the stems to the same length. The width of the handtied should be roughly the same as the height. This will give good proportions. I like to hold the bouquet sideways, keeping the stems tight together and then cut straight across. Secateurs are ideal for this if you have strong stems.

h) Tap the stem ends on a hard surface so that the bouquet will stand (optional).

Variation on the finishing touch

Long-lasting, strong green leaves can create a simple but effective 'frill' around your handtied. *Aspidistra, Cordyline, Fatsia* or small palm leaves are ideal. If you are using the longer *Aspidistra* or *Cordyline* leaves, simply bring the point of the leaf down to the top of the stem and, with a length of florists' tape, wrap the two together to create a loop (see page 212). You will need 7–12 stems depending on the size of your bouquet. Add these to the handtied. You may prefer to tie your bouquet, then add your frill of leaves and tie again (right). For a softer look, incorporate some *Asparagus* fern in the frill (as above).

Adding tissue paper

1 Cut an A4 size piece of tissue or wrapping fabric and place on a similar-sized piece of cellophane.

2 Fold diagonally offset so that there are two peaks at the top. If the handtied is small, one wrap should go around completely but medium or large bouquets will need two wraps.

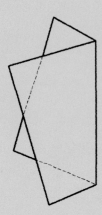 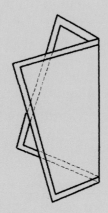 

3 Wrap the folded tissue and cellophane around the tied design and take adhesive tape firmly around where it meets the stems. If using two wraps, secure the first before incorporating the second.

4 Tape or staple the sides near the top of the wrapping.

left A handtied bouquet of roses, *Hyacinthus*, *Hypericum* and *Tulipa* wrapped and secured with one section of tissue and cellophane.

right Here the second section of tissue and cellophane encircles the bouquet. An aquapack containing water has been added and the whole finished with a tie of raffia.

Creating an aquapack

Stem ends form a seal immediately they have been removed from water. Creating an aquapack is the ideal way to transport your flowers so that the recipient need only transfer the flowers to a vase or enjoy as they are. If placing in a vase I think they look better if the twine is first removed.

Method

1 Pre-cut a length of garden twine. Cut a square of strong cellophane. To create a circle of cellophane from a square fold the square into a triangle and then a second triangle. Repeat until you have a tight cone of cellophane. Take sharp scissors and cut a gentle half-circle about halfway down the cellophane. Unfold and you will have a decorative circle.

2 Place the handtied centrally on the cellophane and ensure it keeps firm contact with the stem ends. If the stems are widely splayed, tighten your hold so they come closer together.

3 Draw the four corners of the cellophane up around the flowers and bring them in at the tying point of your handtied or just above. Allow no excess air to enter, which would create air pockets, and make sure that the stem ends remain in contact with the cellophane. Tie with twine. Add ribbon or raffia to finish.

4 Take a jug of water and pour gently through the centre of the handtied.

5 When placing the flowers in a vase, remove the cellophane and ties. Recut the stems on a slant. The spiral will stay in place.

above
Eryngium (sea holly),
spray *Chrysanthemum*
'Kermit', green
Trachelium, pink spray
Chrysanthemum and
tulips.

above and left A handtied of roses, tulips, *Hypericum* with *Betula* (birch) twigs showing the spiralled stems before being placed in a vase. I always prefer to cut the twine from the handtied before placing in water.

right White *Genista* (broom) mixes harmoniously with stocks, *Eustoma* (lisianthus), *Eryngium* (sea holly), spray *Chrysanthemum* 'Kermit' and roses.

The classic style of flower arranging is typically English and has everlasting appeal. It developed at a time when an abundance of flowers could be picked from the garden, but it can still be enjoyed today with florists' flowers and foliage.

It is the basis on which to develop your designing skills, because its geometric formulae – triangles, circles and so on – enable you to gain confidence by following guidelines that lead to effortless success. Classic design provides the stepping stones to understanding and creating contemporary work. As with art, the best contemporary artists study the masters before developing their own style.

CHAPTER 5
CLASSIC DESIGN

Characteristics

- The different designs are all loosely based on a geometric form.
- In each design, every stem radiates – or appears to radiate – from a central point.
- The colours, forms and textures are 'woven' to lead the eye gently through, which brings rhythm to the design.
- There is space between each element of plant material to show every form to its best advantage.

- There is a dominant area at the base of the tallest stem, approximately two-thirds of the way down the design. This can be achieved with larger forms, stronger colour or the use of a different texture.
- There are no strong surprises or contrasts. Variation is soft and gradual.
- The container is sometimes hidden, or of classic design.

left The colours, forms and textures of the *Aeonium* succulent, *Anthurium*, *Sedum*, berries and roses are woven through the design with the plant material radiating from a central area.

below Classic proportions of roses and *Hypericum* with soft and gentle contrasts.

General guidelines

The following guidelines will help you to create successful classic designs. They are not rules, but tips that work and will increase your confidence.

- Foliage is generally used to create the outline, which is then reinforced by other plant material.
- For the foliage outline, make sure that there is approximately the same space or distance between each stem before you add any flowers. This is really important to give a good balanced structure and this point will be reiterated many times throughout this chapter!
- All stems should appear to radiate from an area in the centre of the *exposed* foam, referred to as area **X** in the illustrations on the following pages. The stems do not actually originate from this point (or you would have too many criss-crossing in a small piece of foam) but their source radiates from this point.

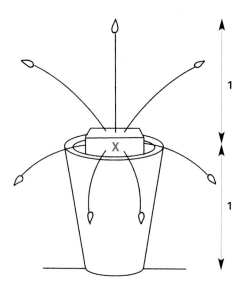

right

top Hard ruscus, the same length as the height of the container once inserted, is placed in the top centre and around the edges of the foam, angled slightly downwards.

middle Further stems of hard ruscus, the same length as above, are angled out of the top of the foam from area **X** to create a gentle dome shape.

bottom Round leaves are added to give interest and a stronger outline. These, and the flowers that follow, are all placed within the initial outline/structure created by the hard ruscus.

- The foam is usually higher than the rim of the container so that plant material can be angled down over the rim, ensuring that the container is an integral part of the design. For small to medium designs the foam should rise above the rim of the container by one-fourth to one-fifth the height of the container. Shave a little foam off at the corners, *very* gently, to soften the shape. This is called chamfering.
- For good visual balance bolder, larger forms, such as *Chrysanthemum*, should be mainly positioned just below the centre of the design but not so low that they appear to be falling out. They should have a leaf positioned beneath them, so that neutral green is at the perimeter.

- The inclusion of round flowers is important as this form holds together all the other elements in the design.
- Arrangements should include some plant material with a smooth texture.
- Give depth and interest to the design by recessing some of the plant material, placing some flowers closer to the foam.
- Insert the minimum length of stem that will keep it securely in position.
- Ensure there is always a reserve of water in the container.

right This simple table design incorporates all the features of classic design. Here, tulips, pink bloom *Chrysanthemum*, green *Chrysanthemum* 'Kermit' and spray roses have been added to the foliage outline shown on the left.

TABLE DESIGNS

Table arrangements include the round, long and low, and tall designs on the pages that follow. This brief introduction informs generally on what to achieve when creating any design for the table. As a rule, arrangements should be tall enough to see under or low enough to see over. In Victorian times, taller arrangements were much in evidence, overflowing with ferns, trails of ivy and a profusion of flowers and fruit. Today the size of our homes – and perhaps the increased pressures in our lives – calls for smaller, lower designs that can be created easily. A height limit of 28 cm (11 in) works well.

For grand occasions, it is fashionable to have an equal mixture of tall and low arrangements for the tables so that there is visual impact on entering the room. Tall candelabras or slim glass vases can hold cascading flowers and foliage on half of the tables, with low designs on the others. The tall containers are usually slim or can be seen through so that the view opposite is not obscured.

Whatever the event, the arrangement should be in good proportion to the size of the table. As a rough guide, no more than one-fifth of the table should be covered. If the table is rectangular and for more than eight people, two or three designs or a slim run of flowers down the centre would be more practical and can be enjoyed by all.

Plant material should be in perfect condition, because it will be seen at close quarters. Choose flowers that will harmonise with the china and table linen. If the occasion is grand, more sophisticated flowers, such as orchids and lilies, may be preferable to humble carnations. If the setting is informal – perhaps in a kitchen – choose flowers such as daisy chrysanthemums and perhaps introduce fruit and vegetables. While visually exciting, ripe fruit can give off ethylene gas, which may shorten the life of a flower arrangement.

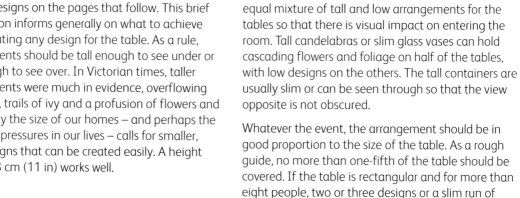

left This low design of tulips in a round glass bowl with lily grass entwined within is ideal for the table with or without the candles and bulbs in the votive containers.

right White *Dendrobium* orchids spiral around the vases in these magnificent table designs by Robbie Honey. The vases sit on a base of white carnations.

above Yellow roses, daisy-like *Matricaria* and ivory *Hypericum* berries

Round table design

As a flower arranger, you will probably create round table designs more frequently than any other style. They can be made with expensive, exotic blooms, or garden or hedgerow flowers to create the required mood at the appropriate cost – be it for Kensington Palace or a fund-raising event at the village hall. Flowers will always make an event more special.

The four table arrangements shown on pages 156–161 all have the same foliage background of hard ruscus but the use of different containers, colours and flowers creates four very different designs. They all include roses as the round flower but there is a wealth of other round flowers which could also be used, such as carnations, dahlias or mini *Gerbera*. The round flowers are complemented by a spray form. A further flower of choice, according to colour and season, completes the design.

below White *Rosa* 'Avalanche', *Eustoma* (lisianthus) and spray roses with *Galax* leaves and a few sprigs of rosemary to provide fragrance as well as textural contrast.

Method

1 Soak the foam for 40–60 seconds, depending on size, then place it in the dish. Secure it well using either a frog and fix or florists' tape or both for larger designs (see page 53). As a rough guideline, if you are using a small to medium container, the foam should rise one quarter to one fifth of the height of the container above the rim. If the container tapers to the base you may simply be able to wedge in the foam so that it is secure. If using tape, pinch it between the fingers so that the tape takes less space over the foam. Gently shave off the four top edges of the foam so that it has a rounder form. Allow sufficient space around the foam so that water can be easily added.

Round table design

You will need

- low, round, watertight container. The green plastic dishes on page 53 would work well but the current trend is to arrange flowers for the home in something a bit more upmarket, such as a terracotta pot, china bowl or ceramic container. For your first attempts, this could be about 12 cm (5 in) in diameter and about 12 cm (5 in) high. This will create an arrangement for a table for about six people. If your container is porous line it with a piece of plastic sheet cut from a refuse sack before you insert your wet foam.

- piece of floral foam. A third of a brick is a good approximate size.
- foam holder (frog) and fix and/or florists' tape
- outline foliage. This could be *Eucalyptus*, ivy, *Gaultheria* (salal tips), *Ligustrum* (privet), *Ribes* (flowering currant) or hard ruscus.
- 7–9 round leaves such as ivy, geranium or *Galax* from the florist. Round leaves are not essential. If they are difficult to find, create a stronger outline with more line foliage.
- 5–7 round flowers such as *Dahlia*, mini *Gerbera* or *Helianthus* (sunflower) roses or chrysanthemums
- spray flowers such as *Alstroemeria*, *Gypsophila*, *Hypericum*, *Viburnum tinus* or spray chrysanthemums
- third type of flower, either round or spray. Not always necessary if you have plenty of flowers. As an alternative you could add snippets of variegated foliage.

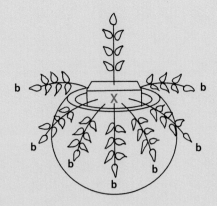

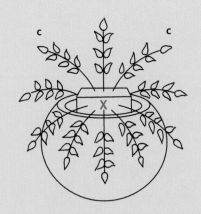

2 Place a stem of foliage centrally in the foam, in position **a**. The stem should be the height of the container plus half the height of the foam above the rim. Once you have placed the stem in the foam the length of the stem will be approximately the same height as the container.

Tip

There is frequently a temptation to have the stem longer than mentioned in step (2), but if the first stem is much longer it will upset the proportions.

left *Rosa* 'Sweet Avalanche', white *Eustoma* (lisianthus) and delicate spray *Bouvardia*.

3 Place stems in position **b**. These will be the same length or slightly shorter than stem **a**. This will depend on the amount of the foam, in the container – the larger the piece of foam, the shorter the stems as the foam will extend further. The first few times you create this design use the same type of plant foliage for all these placements as it will be easier to get a regular shape. Insert stems about half way up the foam that is above the rim, angled slightly downwards over the container, making them appear to originate from the area marked **X**. This is very important. If the stems are angled too sharply downwards they will appear to be falling out. If placed at right angles to the rim of the container, then your arrangement will appear to sit on the container and look awkward.

Tip

It can be difficult to gauge how many stems to use. A rough guideline is to use sufficient stems so that the leaves closest to the foam almost touch the ones next to them.

4 At the top of the foam, place an odd number of stems **c**, which should be the same length as **a**. The line drawing shows two stems **c** but you will need more. Avoid placing them directly above the material that you have already inserted – place them in between. They should all appear to come from area **X**. The overall form of your arrangement should be a gentle dome, which is wider at the base than the top. Avoid placing the stems out of the edges or corners of the foam. There should be more or less equal space between each stem of foliage.

5 If you have round leaves, add them now. Avoid creating a static effect by inserting the stems so that the leaves lie at different angles. Keep the stems long so that you reinforce the outline rather than trying to hide the foam by cutting them short. At this point you will be able to see a small amount of foam but it should not be obvious.

6 Position your round flowers through the foliage outline. Your first flower placement should reinforce the central stem and be upright. (If it is angled away from this central vertical position, it will be difficult to achieve a symmetrical design.) Try not to go beyond the outline created by your foliage. Again, all stems should appear to radiate from area **X**.

Tip

Keep lifting your arrangement to eye level to check that plant material flows down over the rim of the container.

Tip

Many people worry about odd and even numbers but no one notices if there are more than six flowers! In fact if you are creating a symmetrical design an even number is often better than odd as you will establish the symmetry with the placement of a flower top centre. You are then left with perhaps three or five flowers to distribute through the design rather than an even number.

7 Add your other flowers and berries to complete. If they are light and airy, such as *Chamelaucium* (waxflower), *Gypsophila* or *Solidago* (golden rod) you can go a little beyond the established framework without upsetting the balance or proportions.

8 Ensure that your container always has a reservoir of water.

Variations

- Wrap wide double-sided tape around the outside of a plastic bowl. Adhere large flat leaves such as *Cocculus*, ivy or *Prunus* (laurel) to the tape to cover the bowl.
- Wrap long trails of well-conditioned ivy around each other to create a circle slightly larger than the rim of the container. Rest on the rim of the container to add interest.
- Fill a basket or attractive container with a mass of fruiting tree ivy to cover the foam. Then simply add an array of flowers in colours of your choice among the ivy.
- Add a candle centrally.
- Fruit and vegetables add interest to table arrangements and are very simple to incorporate. Take wooden cocktail or kebab sticks. Impale two or three lengths (depending on the weight of the produce) into the fruit or vegetable and add to the arrangement.

right Peach roses combined with *Hypericum* berries and spray roses.

Long and low table design

This arrangement is suitable for an oval or rectangular table. Its shape can also be easily adapted for a top table or mantelpiece.

below A long and low design ideal for a top table. It would also work well on a window or mantelpiece ledge. The outline of *Eucalyptus cinerea* and *E. parvifolia* is reinforced with leather leaf and *Galax* leaves. Frilly tulips take colour out to the edges of the design. Red roses give strength and *Hypericum* 'Coco Grande' and spray roses complete the picture.

Long and low table design with summer flowers

You will need

- third, half or full brick of foam (depending on the length of the arrangement you wish to create)
- shallow container. The foam must fill no more than two-thirds of the container (so that a water reservoir can be added) and rise above the rim. A plastic foam tray or a plant saucer, widely available from DIY stores and garden centres, is ideal as it can be easily hidden by the plant material.
- outline foliage such as small-leaved ivy sprays, *Danae racemosa* (soft ruscus), *Eucalyptus*, *Fagus* (beech), *Gaultheria* (salal tips) or *Hebe*
- round leaves to give a smooth texture such as ivy, x *Fatshedera* or *Galax*. These may not be needed if the outline foliage already has a smooth texture.
- line flowers such as larkspur, *Matthiola* (stocks), *Dendrobium* (Singapore orchids) or *Liatris*
- round flowers such as carnations, *Dahlia*, peonies or open roses
- filler flowers such as *Alchemilla mollis* (lady's mantle), *Genista* (broom), *Limonium* (statice) or *Solidago* (golden rod).

Method

1 Place the foam (soaked, as described on page 44) in the dish and secure well. Place a stem of outline foliage centrally, in position **a**, as shown below. For your first attempt, use foliage that rises about 12.5 cm (5 in) above the level of the foam. Place two stems, of the same line plant material, in both long ends of the foam, **b**, each approximately 15 cm (6 in) long. These should be placed halfway down the exposed foam. You have now formed the triangle **XYZ**. Stem **b** can be a length of your choice, but they should be roughly the same.

2 Place a short length of foliage in position **c**, halfway down the exposed foam, and repeat on the other side. The length will depend upon the desired width of design. Consider the shape you have created to be an oval and add two more stems each side to maintain this, **d**. Ensure that every stem appears to originate from area **X**. All the lower placements should have approximately the same spacing.

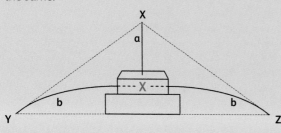

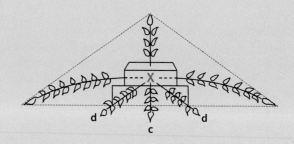

3 Place an odd number of stems, **e**, in the top of the foam. At this point, do not allow any material to protrude outside the dotted-line triangle **XYZ** (point 1). Once again, check that all stems appear to come from area **X**.

4 Add more foliage to give a strong outline, including a few round leaves if they are available. Make sure there is approximately the same space or distance between each stem so that the design is well balanced.

5 Add line flowers almost to the limit of the design and throughout. Place the first flower so that it reinforces the first vertical placement of the foliage. Put the stems at regular intervals to avoid wide empty spaces. Pay particular attention to the areas between placements **b** and **d**. Add extra outline material if needed to give a smoother flow.

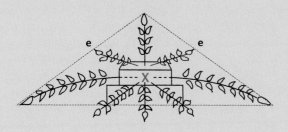

6 Place the round flowers at intervals through the arrangement. Avoid creating an all-round arrangement with two arms attached. If the focal flowers are of differing sizes place the smallest focal flowers closer to the edges, the largest in the centre and the others in between.

7 Add spray material to complete. Try to keep within the framework established by the plant material, though delicate plants such as *Alchemilla mollis* (lady's mantle) or *Genista* (broom) can extend beyond without upsetting the balance. Keep bolder plant material within the set boundaries.

8 Ensure that there is water in the bottom of your container.

above This design was created in a strip of low plastic rectangular trays placed end to end and filled with *Hydrangea*, *Eustoma* roses and *Symphoricarpos* (snowberry). It was positioned on the edge of the top table at a wedding reception.

below This long, low arrangement in a bark container would be ideal for a mantelpiece design at Christmas. The candle was first positioned in the centre of the foam, which was then covered with ivy, *Dorycnium hirsutum* (hairy canary clover), *Rosa* 'Avalanche', wired pine cones and wooden stars.

Variations

- Use for a mantelpiece or top table with the addition of flexible plant material such as trails of ivy that will soften the harsh edge of the mantel or table.
- A design for the top of a coffin is created in exactly the same way, but you must ensure that it is no taller than 28 cm (11 in), so that it will fit into the hearse.
- A strip of flowers can be created by filling several containers with foam (removing angled corners of foam so that water can be added) and placing them end to end. Cover the foam with short lengths of foliage and add your flowers. Be sure to incorporate a flower with a round form.

below and right Slim containers holding foam were placed along the centre of the table and covered with a base of *Gaultheria* (salal tips). Gorgeous white *Hydrangea*, *Freesia*, roses and *Solidago* were cut short and arranged through the foliage, along with stubborn lilies which had to be appreciated for their gracious green buds alone!

Tall table design

This tall arrangement is suitable for a buffet table. It is often used as a table centrepiece when strong visual impact is required on entry to the room.

below Tall lily vases on mirror glass hold a posy pad with additional foam (see page 170). *Eucalyptus cinerea* and *Parthenocissus tricuspidata* leaves (Boston ivy) create the outline, which is then complemented by *Hydrangea*, roses, *Eustoma* and *Ozothamnus diosmifolius* (rice flower – the pink spray flower), which is invaluable during its short season. The berries are pink *Symphoricarpos* (snowberry).

Tall table design for late summer

You will need

- container 70–90 cm (28–35 in) tall. It needs to have sufficient height above the eye level of the seated guests and to be slim or see-through (such as glass), so that the view across the table is not totally obscured. It could be a tall glass lily vase.
- a) 25 cm (10 in) posy pad with a polystyrene base, a third of a brick of foam and wire hairpins
  or
  b) candlecup or tapered dish or bowl that fits securely in the tall container's opening, florists' fix, foam holder and/or tape and a piece of foam
- line foliage with a natural curve such as soft ruscus or *Eucalyptus*
- line/spray fruits or flowers such as *Symphoricarpos* (snowberry), *Ozothamnus diosmifolius* (rice flower) or *Eustoma* (lisianthus) rather than rigid stems
- round flowers such as open roses, small *Hydrangea* or mini *Gerbera*
- other spray flowers of choice such as *Aster, Hypericum* or *Solidago*.

Method

1 Fill the container with water to give ballast. The water can be coloured with food dye if you so wish.

2 a) If you are using the posy pad (see drawing below left a), place this on top of the container and press, so that the opening indents the foam. Take a knife and score the pad around the outside of the outline. The pad will now fit securely on top of the container. If additional security is needed, place florists' fix around the rim of the container. Wet the foam pad. Now take a third of a brick of wet foam and attach it to the centre of the posy pad with long wire hairpins. This will give additional height to the centre of the arrangement.

or

b) If you are using a tapered dish or candlecup (see drawing right b) adhere a foam holder to the base with florists' fix. Place a piece of soaked foam on the foam holder. Add tape if you wish. For additional security you may want to place florists' fix around the rim of the

tall container. If the container is glass, and you are using a candlecup, you may need to add coloured water or sisal in the vase to hide the protrusion. Alternatively make sure the protrusion is concealed by plant material angled downwards.

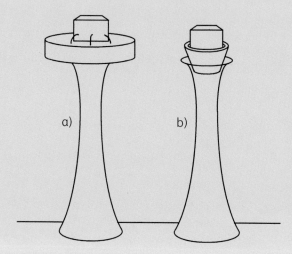

a)   b)

3 Place a stem of foliage centrally in the top of the foam **a**. Take further lengths of foliage and angle them downwards out of the sides. These should be of different lengths to give interest. Do not angle the stems so sharply that they appear to be falling out, or insufficiently so that the arrangement seems to be perched on the stand, **b**.

4 Take further stems and angle out of the top of the foam, **c**.

5 Make a stronger, fuller shape with your line foliage. At this point there should be a uniform distance between each stem. Add some plain, smooth leaves for contrast and interest. *Parthenocissus tricuspidata* (Boston ivy) leaves are everywhere in the summer and autumn and are ideal. As an alternative try small *Hosta* leaves or ivy.

6 Reinforce the foliage outline with flowers which have flexibility or a curve in their stems, such as *Dendrobium* (Singapore orchid) or *Eustoma* (lisianthus). Place the first flower stem centrally (this will only be short). Continue placing other flowers throughout the design.

7 Add the round flowers. Fill in with your spray flowers and any additional foliage.

right In this tall design of hanging *Amaranthus*, roses, *Hydrangea*, peonies, *Dendrobium* orchids and *Viburnum opulus*, slices of lime hide the mechanics. Flowers and fruit are scattered at the base of the vase to give visual interest at a different level.

Variations

- Add a posy ring at the base and cover with flowers and foliage (see Ring design page 190). Ensure you place the ring in position before you start to decorate.
- Position on a circle of mirror glass and add five votive holders around the base of the stand linked with petals that match the flowers in the design.
- For a buffet table where there is no concern about blocking a view, fill the vase with fruit or vegetables, pasta, shells, aggregates or coloured water.

THE CLASSICS

Classics are timeless – fashions may come and go but the designs you will see on the following pages have stood the test of time. Understanding these designs will provide you with the basics from which you can grow in experience and knowledge.

Symmetrical triangle

The classic symmetrical triangle holds and displays plant material to its best advantage from three sides. Today, this design is seen less frequently but it is still the essential shape for pedestals, on view so often in large, open areas such as churches and hotels as well as in competitions. It is by far the most effective way of displaying an abundance of plant material that is to be enjoyed by a large audience. As it is a symmetrically balanced design it needs to be placed centrally on a sideboard or table or in a niche.

Key points for arranging the symmetric triangle

- The container must be integrated into the design. This is achieved by angling plant material down over the rim and the top of the container so that one flows into the other. The container can be a low bowl or dish that is hidden or a tall decorative container that is part of the design.
- Allow your flowers to face all directions to achieve maximum interest. Look at a plant and observe how the flowers and leaves do this. All angles of flowers are interesting and a combination of angles gives variety.
- *Gerbera* or mini *Gerbera* and other dominant round flowers should be placed at various angles to give variety and interest.

- Try not to create a flat arrangement. Depth or a strong three-dimensional form will hold the eye. Depth can be created in different ways:

  - The back of your arrangement should be built up with foliage and flowers, even though it may be close to a wall. This will give better balance. They do not have to be the choicest of your blooms.
  - Recess some of your flowers and foliage. Shorter stems, usually of bolder material, are positioned closer to the foam. Recessing also reduces a 'stem-heavy' effect, which is often created by using flowers that have a small flower head in proportion to stem (carnations, for instance).

below A study in pink. *Rosa* 'Sweet Avalanche', *Eustoma* (lisianthus), mini *Gerbera* and *Freesia* combined with green *Trachelium* on a base of *Eucalyptus*.

Classic symmetrical triangle design

You will need

- raised container
- foam to fit your container. This can be wedged into the opening (ensure there is room for a reservoir of water), or it could be secured with a foam holder and fix and/or a length of florists' tape.
- line foliage such as *Gaultheria* (salal tips). The plant material should not be too finely linear, because you need to create a strong structure without using too many stems, which would look fussy.
- smooth-textured leaves such as *Fatsia*, *Galax*, *Hosta* or ivy with leaves that are rounder in form rather than linear
- line flowers such as *Liatris*, *Antirrhinum*, small bridal *Gladiolus* or larkspur
- round flowers such as *Dianthus* (carnations), roses or mini *Gerbera*
- spray material such as spray roses, waxflower, *Alstroemeria* or *Hypericum* berries.

Method

1 Place a stem of line material **a** that is about one and a half times the height of the container into the top of the foam centrally and two-thirds of the way back. This stem should not lean forward but very slightly backwards.

2 Place two stems **b** two-thirds the length of **a** sideways out of the central part of the exposed foam, angled slightly forward and downwards. This flow of plant material extending below the rim of the container prevents the arrangement looking awkward on the container. A gentle curve to the plant material will make this design look more natural. You have now created the triangle **XYZ**.

3 Add two stems **c**, approximately half the length of stem **a**, out of the top of the foam. They should not protrude outside the triangle's boundary. If they do go beyond, they must be reduced – even if they are less than half the length of **a**.

4 Now check that all stems appear to originate from the area **X** deep in the foam and all are equidistant from each other.

5 Add two short stems **d** about one-third the length of **a**, at the front of the design, angled slightly downwards and outwards.

6 Give depth to the design by adding a stem of foliage and/or flowers **e** behind the central stem. This will be shorter than the main stem and angled slightly backwards. Place a short stem in the centre of the foam angled forwards **f**. At this point check that there is approximately the same distance between each stem.

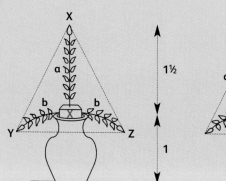

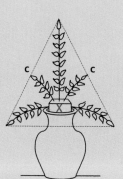

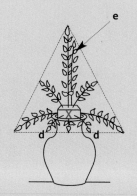

right The outline structure for this raised triangular design was made with *Gaultheria* (salal tips) and round *Galax* leaves. Linear purple *Liatris* takes colour through. Vintage *Dianthus* creates strong focal form and is complemented by mini *Anthurium*, spray roses and waxflower.

7 Use smooth-textured large single leaves to cover some of the foam. Select some with longer stems so that they are not all at the base of the design, but are taken through the central two-thirds of the triangle. Check that the design is balanced – side to side of the central axis from front to back and from top to bottom.

8 Reinforce the shape with line flowers, but do not go beyond the boundaries of the triangle. Take additional line flowers through the design, front and back.

9 Create the focal area with round flowers in the central two-thirds of the arrangement. Do not place your focal flowers too neatly. Turn them to show off all their angles and give interest.

10 Complete the design with filler flowers and foliage.

Variation on the symmetrical triangle – the pedestal

The typical pedestal uses a large amount of plant material and therefore needs a strong plinth or stand to present the flowers and foliage to advantage.

Suggestions for plant material

Line foliage

Fagus (beech), *Camellia*, *Cornus* (dogwood), *Ribes* (flowering currant) and *Rhododendron* are excellent as line material and create a full outline simply and inexpensively.

Large smooth-textured foliage

Smooth-textured leaves could be *Aspidistra*, *Cordyline*, *Fatsia* or *Hosta*.

Fatsia

Line flowers

Line flowers could be *Antirrhinum*, *Delphinium*, *Gladiolus*, *Molucella leavis* (bells of Ireland) or stocks.

Gladiolus

Focal flowers

Hydrangeas are the ideal focal flower – readily available from mid-summer to late autumn. Alternatively try *Anthurium*, bloom *Chrysanthemum*, *Gerbera or* sunflowers.

Hydrangea

Spray flowers

Alstroemeria, lilies or *Solidago* work well as spray material.

Alstroemeria

Mechanics for large-scale designs

Jumbo foam is ideal because it has a heavier density and is thus able to support heavier stems than standard foam. Jumbo block can be placed in the plastic bowl without further support, because it is very heavy once full of water. If you are using two bricks of floral foam, place one upright on a frog at the back of the bowl. The second brick can be positioned sideways in front of the first brick. Use any excess that you have sliced off to wedge the foam firmly in position. The foam needs to rise well above the rim of the container. A good guideline is that the foam should be twice as high above the rim as the height of the bowl. Leave space within the bowl so you can add water. You will be using lots of plant material so water will need to be added regularly.

below: A magnificent pedestal created to celebrate the life of the great flower arranger Julia Clements by Susan Philips. Soft ruscus creates the outline and *Aspidistra* gives smooth contrast. White *Delphinium*, pink larkspur, purple stocks and white *Antirrhinum* reinforce this outline, while roses and carnations give round focal interest. Spray *Eustoma* (lisianthus) complete the design.

Classic pedestal

You will need

- green plastic bulb bowl, or a small, round washing-up bowl. A bowl approximately 20 cm (8 in) wide and 10 cm (4 in) deep is ideal for a moderate-size pedestal.
- piece of OASIS® Jumbo foam (see page 178), or two standard bricks of foam
- length of 2.5 cm (1 in) mesh chicken wire to reinforce your mechanics. This is only needed if you wish to create a very large pedestal and you are not using Jumbo foam. Cut the amount needed to make a cap over your foam. Keep it in place with reel wire, florists' tape or large rubber bands. If you are using rubber bands, interloop them under the bowl and bring them up over the foam and wire to secure.
- bold plant material in scale with the stand and situation.

Method

Follow the numbered steps 1–10 for the symmetrical triangle, but ensure that your plant material drapes copiously downwards, all the way round, to give depth and movement. Your first central placement will establish the finished size of your pedestal design. It can be as tall as you want. The length of all the other outline stems will relate proportionally to the length of the first stem. If the scale is large place three or more stems, rather than two, to come forward at the bottom.

right A classic front-facing pedestal. Beech is the ideal outline for pedestals during the summer months. *Aspidistra* leaves are available all year round and provide a smooth plane against which flowers show to advantage. *Delphinium* give linear interest from their tips down into the centre of the design. *Hydrangea* and roses give strength through their round form. Spray *Eustoma* (lisianthus) and white *Symphoricarpos* (snowberry) provide additional interest.

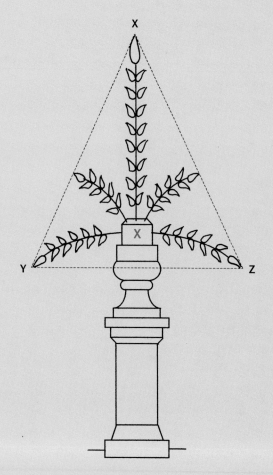

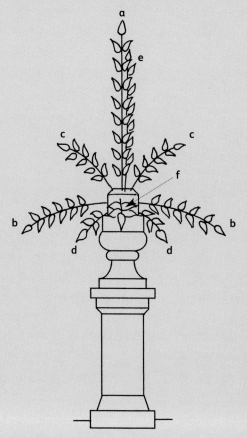

Asymmetric triangle

The asymmetric triangle is one of the most pleasing classic designs. It is usually positioned on one side of a chest, mantelpiece, altar or table rather than centrally. It is often used to balance an ornament or lamp.

In contrast, in symmetric design, the two sides positioned on the left and right of the central axis are more or less the same in terms of visual weight.

below Tall *Eremurus* create the height in this asymmetric design. *Hosta* leaves provide weight to the short side of the triangle. *Helenium* and marigolds create strong focal interest, with the *Dianthus barbatus* (sweet William) complementing the other forms.

In asymmetric design the design is balanced on one side by bolder , shorter plant material and on the other by finer, longer plant material.

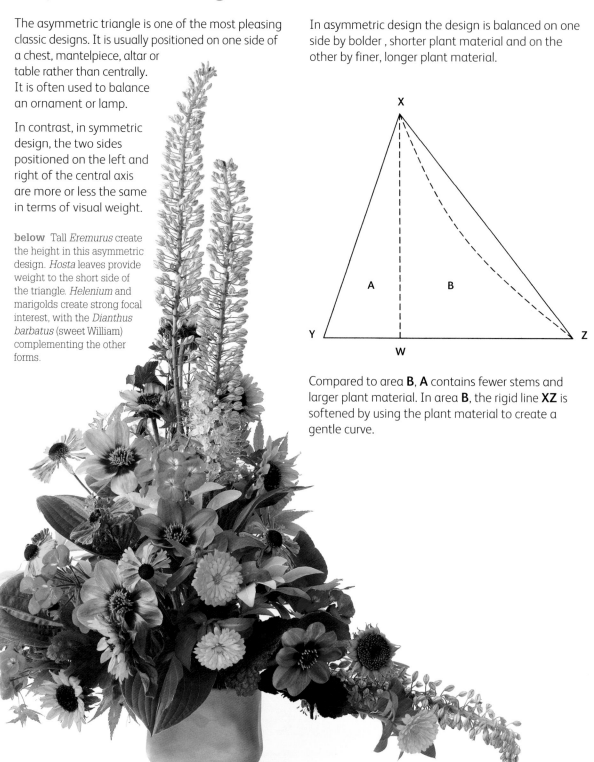

Compared to area **B**, **A** contains fewer stems and larger plant material. In area **B**, the rigid line **XZ** is softened by using the plant material to create a gentle curve.

Asymmetric triangle

You will need

- low bowl, or one that is slightly raised.
- foam – one-third of a brick is ample. Gently chamfer the top edges and corners.
- foam holder and fix and/or florists' tape.
- line material – the tallest stem, which will establish the height, should have a gentle curve, such as broom, *Eremurus*, *Escallonia*, *Eucalyptus*, holly or ivy.
- strong, large smooth-textured leaves such as *Bergenia*, *Hosta* or x *Fatshedera*.
- round flowers such as *Rudbeckia*, marigolds, *Cosmos* and *Dahlia*.
- spray flowers such as *Alchemilla mollis*, *Phlox* or *Solidago*.

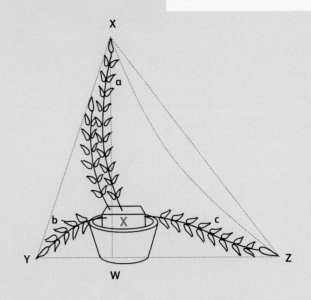

Method

1 Place the tallest stem, **a**, in the top of the foam, two thirds of the way back and slightly to one side. Angle the stem so that the tip is approximately above the spot where the stem enters the foam. Do not allow the stem tip to go beyond the centre of the foam, or it will look as if it is falling over.

2 Place line material, **b**, one-third the length of **a** out of the front of the foam angled slightly downwards over the rim of the container.

3 Place line material, **c**, two-thirds the length of **a**, out of the side of the foam and slightly forwards. You have now formed the triangle **XYZ** divided by the line **XW**. Triangle **XYW** (area **A**) will contain your heavier material while triangle **XWZ** (area **B**) will contain the finer material (see diagram on the left). Add further line material to create a stronger structure.

4 Use larger leaves to cover the mechanics. Use them particularly in the narrow triangle **XYW** to give weight and strength to that side of the design. Remember that all stems should appear to radiate from area **X**. Graduate the size of the plant material carefully so that the design is a harmonious whole and does not have an arm sticking out ungracefully.

5 Reinforce the outline with line flowers. Position them at different angles throughout, building up a strong three-dimensional effect. Give a gentle scoop to the long side of the triangle **XWZ** to incorporate more space around the design.

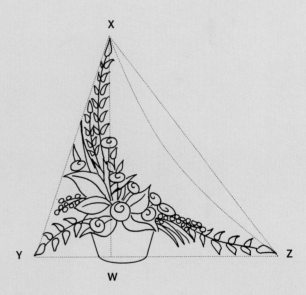

6 Use round flowers to create the area of strongest interest. For good balance, this is located around the base of the tallest stem, about two-thirds of the way down. Graduate others away from the centre.

7 Use spray material to complete the design. Do not worry if a small amount of foam is showing at the back. You may wish to cut some filler material very short and use it to cover the gaps. Create depth and interest without destroying your shape by angling some material backwards, particularly in the deepest part of your scoop.

Downward crescent

The downward crescent is light and graceful. It gives a sophisticated arrangement using a minimal amount of plant material. As the downward crescent is arranged in a raised container it can be placed where space is at a premium. You can use a bottle, candlestick or tall, slim container. A bottle can be filled with water to give extra stability.

Try to find a container that is between 25 cm (10 in) and 35 cm (14 in) high. An arrangement on a 25 cm (10 in) high container will use smaller-sized material than an arrangement on a container 35 cm (14 in) high. Trails of neat ivy, pinks, florists' roses and *Alchemilla mollis* would be in scale with the smaller container but larger ivies and generous garden roses would be more appropriate for the taller one.

A candlecup should be securely attached to your container with florists' fix and florists' tape.

Elegant downward crescent

You will need

- piece of foam. The foam should rise about 2.5 cm (1 in) above the rim of the container or candlecup.
- a tall container, candlestick or bottle.
- candlecup (see page 58) or a dish that will fit securely in the container's opening.
- candle (optional), cocktail sticks and tape.
- curved line material (this design will not work with straight line material) such as *Eucalyptus*, *Dendrobium* (Singapore orchids), honeysuckle, lengths of ivy or *Genista* (broom).
- round leaves such as round *Galax*, *Heuchera*, ivy leaves, *Parthenocissus tricuspidata* (Boston ivy) or *Pelargonium* (geranium).
- round flowers such as open roses, marigolds or mini *Gerbera*.
- spray material such as *Alchemilla mollis*, *Alstroemeria*, x *Solidaster* or *Viburnum tinus*.

Method

1 Place the foam in the candlecup or dish and secure well.

2 If using a candle, prepare as on page 58 and insert in the centre of the foam.

3 Insert a length of line material **a** centrally. If using a candle it should be no more than half the length of the candle. Stem **a** is short. On a 25 cm (10 in) tall container the tallest stem would be about 10 cm (4 in) and no more. This is a crescent and the finished design should have the form of a crescent moon.

left In this arrangement curving stems of *Dendrobium* (Singapore orchids) create the outline rather than flexible line foliage such as soft ruscus or *Eucalyptus*. *Chrysanthemum* 'Anastasia' and *Anthurium* blooms give focal interest.

4 Insert curved outline material **b** into the centre of each side of the foam so that it flows downwards. You have now formed the shape **XYZ**. If straightened, stems **b** will be approximately the same length as the container's height. The curve in the stem and the angle at which they are placed will mean they fall well short of the base.

5 Add shorter stems, **c**, also angled downwards. Their stem ends should appear to have the same imaginary origin, area **X**. Repeat on the far side. These should be about one-third the length of placements **b**. They should just reach over the rim of the container and a little beyond.

6 Insert short stems **d** in the top of the foam, all apparently arising from the same area in the foam, **X**. Each stem should be equidistant from the next.

7 Use plain, round concealer leaves to hide the mechanics and to provide a restful contrast to the other material. A relatively large leaf placed low and centrally will complement a focal flower.

8 Insert your focal flowers. The larger flowers should be placed in the central area, graduating outwards to the smallest flowers. If the arrangement is to be placed against a wall, use your best blooms at the front.

9 Add filler material to complete the design. As in the oval table arrangement, ensure that the two long stems are not isolated. Graduate the material so that the design has unity. Do not worry if you feel that only a little is needed – you are probably right.

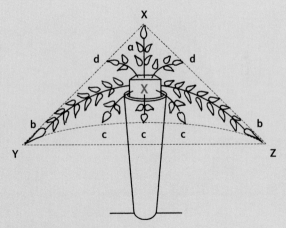

Upward crescent

The upward crescent is a stylised but effective design that uses only a small amount of plant material. Unlike the classic downward crescent, which has sides of approximately the same length, the upward crescent often looks better when one side is longer than the other. It is usual to follow a generous curve of the new moon.

This design cannot be created without curved line material, so if you cannot find any, create another style of arrangement. However, some plant material can be encouraged to curve. Broom can be soaked for a couple of hours and then tied in the required shape. When dried it will be permanently curved, but make sure you do not overdo it or else you will find you have created a circle. Blossom is ideal as it takes colour and flowers to the limits of the design without the addition of extra stems which can muddle the outline. *Chaenomeles* (flowering japonica or quince) often has lovely curves. Flexible plant material such as willow or dogwood can be encouraged to bend using warm hands.

The plant material needs to be kept firmly in place and although you can use foam, a pinholder is recommended. If the stems are in foam they can swing round. A pinholder can easily be covered with plant material, moss or small pebbles. Covering foam can lead to a fussy effect that is bottom-heavy and can destroy the clarity of the overall form.

left A simple and stylish upward crescent by Jenny Bennett. Curving branches provide the silhouette with tulips and two *Arum italicum* leaves at the base. The tulips act as both line and round flowers. The curved stems are longer than those described in the step by step on the right but work well because the stems are bare and give a clean outline.

Simple upward crescent

You will need

- pinholder with a 6.25 cm (2 ½ in) diameter. A larger or smaller pinholder will also work depending on the flowers and foliage you wish to use.
- low, shallow container large enough to take the pinholder and which allows the pins to be covered by water
- some flat pebbles or moss to hide the pinholder (optional)
- curved line material such as branches, *Forsythia*, *Genista* (broom), rosemary, blossom or pussy willow
- large smooth-textured leaves such as *Arum italicum*, *Hosta* or Boston ivy
- line flowers with curved stems such as tulips, Singapore orchids or blossom
- round flowers such as open roses, lilies or tulips
- spray flowers (optional).

Method

1 Place a stem of curved plant material in the pinholder, **a**. This should be approximately twice the length of the shallow container.

2 The second stem of curved material, **b**, should be about one-third the length of **a** but should be placed so that the imaginary dotted line shown in the diagram would approximately complete the circle.

3 If you have used fine stems to create the outline reinforce with shorter stems.

4 Use a few large leaves to help conceal the pinholder. Always bear in mind the clean-cut sickle effect you are creating.

5 Line flowers can reinforce the shape but do not try to do the impossible with stems that are too rigid, such as *Iris*, or with buds that will quickly open and spoil your outline. Line flowers may not be necessary if you are using blossom, flowers or interesting branches for your initial outline.

6 Create the focal area. This should be in the area at the base of the tallest stem. If stem **a** does not come over as far as the centre of the pinholder your focal area may be slightly off-centre. Only use one or two round flowers at this point. If possible place a few smaller flowers and their buds further into the curve to link the outer parts of the design with the centre so that the design is a harmonious whole.

7 If necessary, complete the shape with spray material. This is not always required.

8 Look at your design and remove any pieces of plant material which are superfluous. Check that you do not have an accumulation of leaves at the base which would spoil the smooth line of the curve. Space and a clear-cut outline are very important – less really is more in this design. Cover any mechanics which still show with moss or flat pebbles rather than more plant material.

Hogarth curve

The Hogarth curve is attributed to the artist of the same name, who called it the "line of beauty". It loosely follows the shape of the letter 'S'. It is a stylised shape that most people either love or hate. Creating a successful Hogarth curve gives the arranger a keen sense of achievement. It is a building block in the understanding of the use of plant material and pleases many.

Variation

Try a Hogarth with a wider 'S' shape.

right A Hogarth curve with white *Veronica* reinforcing the curving stems of *Physocarpus opulifolius* 'Diabolo'. *Heuchera* leaves give smooth texture while *Alstroemeria* and starry *Astrantia* complete the picture.

You will need

- tall, raised container at least 25 cm (10 in) high. If a bottle or candlestick is being used a small candlecup or a round plastic dish with a cork glued to the base will be required.
- foam holder and fix
- small amount of foam. It must not fill the candlecup as the more foam used the more plant material will be needed to hide it. This can detract from the smoothness of your shape. It must rise well above the rim.
- curved line foliage such as *Eucalyptus*, *Physocarpus opulifolius* 'Diabolo' or *Ribes sanguineum*
- round leaves such as *Heuchera*, large ivy leaves or *Galax*
- curved line/spray flowers such as *Veronica*
- smooth-textured leaves
- round flowers such as *Cosmos*, *Dahlia*, mini *Gerbera* or roses
- spray flowers (optional) such as *Alstoemeria*, *Astrantia* or waxflower.

Method

1 Place the soaked foam in the candlecup using a foam holder and fix if necessary.

2 The first placement **a** must be curved plant material. It should be about 1¼–1½ times the height of the container and positioned in the side or top of the foam so that the tip of the stem has an imaginary line to the centre of the foam. It should lean very slightly backwards. This will not work unless the first placement is curved. The stem end will appear to originate from area **X**.

3 The second stem must also be of curved plant material. This stem **b** should be approximately one third to one half the length of **a**. It is positioned to come forward towards the viewer. It should appear to be a natural extension of **a**. The stem end is inserted in the side of the foam, or the front, so that it comes forward to create an informal 'S' shape.

4 Position smooth-textured leaves to give a stronger structure but do not cut the stems too short – the objective is not to hide the foam at this stage. If you do it will be difficult to find space in the foam to add further stems. Take care not to detract from your 'S' shape.

5 Line flowers may be added to reinforce the foliage line and to take colour through. Ensure that they are shorter than the foliage and that they follow the shape.

6 Place a round flower at the base of your tallest stem **a**. Other round flowers can be used to graduate the shape carefully towards the extremities but these should be smaller or angled so that they are less dominant.

7 Cover any visible foam with short lengths of spray plant material. Use the minimum amount possible. Do remember that you will be far more conscious of foam showing than anyone else. Fill out your shape. Think of the overall 'S' shape with every placement. You will be thankful that you used the minimum amount of foam – there is less to cover!

Caution!

Do not make the central area too wide.

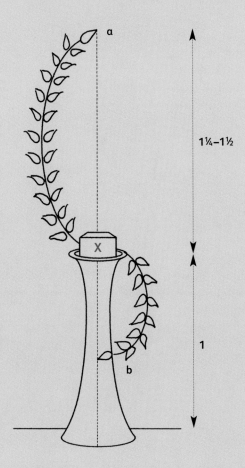

Ring design

This is ideal as a wreath for hanging or as a table centrepiece.

right Blue grey conifer and plain *Heuchera* give the base for a wonderful array of *Viburnum tinus* berries, *Sedum* flowers, *Hydrangea* and *Rosa* 'Cool Water'.

above These rings are incredibly easy to make. Wet a foam ring and cover completely with short snippets of ivy, conifer or *Hydrangea* from the garden. For a more sumptuous look you could use roses or carnations. Hang, or fill with cones, shells, candles, shiny baubles or a tall vase filled with flowers.

left *Ruscus hypophyllum* (hard ruscus) and *Fagus* (copper beech) create a strong background for the individual heads of *Physalis franchettii* (Chinese lanterns) and *Cymbidium* orchid arranged with cream roses and sprays of *Hypericum* berries.

Autumnal ring design

You will need

- floral ring 25 (10 in), 30 cm (12 in) or 35 cm (14 in) in diameter, depending on the size of the table, with either a polystyrene or plastic base
- sharp knife
- foliage to cover the foam. This should include:
  - smooth-textured leaves such as ivy or *Galax*
  - leaves of contrasting textures
  or
  - a mass of one foliage such as *Hedera arborescens* (tree ivy)
- round and spray flowers.

Method

1 Wet the foam by placing on water. This will take about 60 seconds. Take the knife and gently remove the angular edges to the ring.

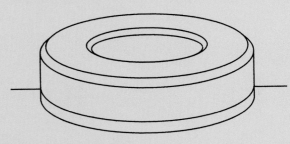

2 Cut short lengths of foliage and cover the foam, being careful to angle the leaves over the rim of the ring, both inwards and outwards. Mix your textures if using more than one type of foliage.

3 Add your round flowers. These need to be placed centrally around the circle. Avoid positioning them too much to either side or the dominant form will encourage the eye to move out of the circle.

4 Fill in with other flowers, berries, fruit or variegated foliage if your flowers are limited.

Variations

- Place a thick church candle or hurricane lamp in the centre
- Position the ring at the base of a candelabra
- Fill the centre with Easter eggs, Christmas baubles or bags of sugared almonds.

above left A ring of sprigs of short conifer is decorated with a few lichen-covered twigs, a few winter *Cyclamen* leaves and a bunch of *Freesia*. The centre has been filled with cones and pomanders for additional fragrance.

below left Sprigs of garden foliage – conifer, *Heuchera*, *Pittosporum* and berries – are highlighted with a few red roses which colour link with the central candle.

below A ring of *Acacia* (mimosa), *Gloriosa superba* 'Rothschildiana' and roses on a base of *Gaultheria* (salal tips) and fluffy ming fern is filled with chocolate eggs for Easter.

$\mathcal{C}$ontemporary design is constantly evolving using new varieties of plant material and old favourites in exciting and innovative ways. New techniques develop, new products are incorporated and trends are established.

Whereas classic design is relatively easy to copy, using step-by-step instructions, contemporary design has its inconsistencies. A strong background in the classics will enable you to look, adapt and perhaps improve on the designs seen in books, magazines, hotels and at shows. Here I explain general characteristics, established techniques and terms, as well as suggesting a few ideas to get you going.

CHAPTER 6
CONTEMPORARY DESIGN

left A simple structure has been created by wrapping wool around wire and then manipulating as appropriate. A bed of *Hydrangea* covers the foam. *Gloriosa superba* 'Rothschildiana' and roses complete the design.

General characteristics

Some or all of the following may be evident:

- Massing/blocking of plant material. A flower or leaf is not always seen individually but as part of a mass of colour, form and texture.
- Exciting and unusual textural contrasts.
- Minimal use of foliage, if at all.
- 'Grass-like' foliage such as *Equisetum hyemele*, flexi grass, bear grass and steel grass.
- Manipulated leaves.
- House plant foliage.
- Limited colour palette. Subtle colour schemes that are often monochromatic.
- Vintage coloured varieties of flowers such as *Hydrangea*, *Dianthus* (carnations) and roses.
- Natural mechanics created from roots, branches and stems.
- Asymmetric balance.
- Containers made from natural plant material such as bark, stems, branches or manipulated leaves.

- Bold feature flowers such as *Anthurium*, *Dianthus* (carnations), *Gloriosa superba* 'Rothschildiana', *Hydrangea*, *Orchida* 'Vanda', *O. Phalaenopsis*, *O. Cymbidium*, large-headed roses and *Zantedeschia* (calla).
- Seasonal flowers and foliage.
- New and interesting varieties of flowers and foliage.
- Flowers that last well out of water
- Succulents such as *Aeonium*, *Echeveria* and *Sempervivum*.
- Accessories such as wool, cable-ties, pegs, decorative wire, Perspex, plastic straws, felt and clay.
- Structures made from natural plant material so that only minimal fresh plant material is needed to create good design.

below Lengths of OASIS®
Rustic Wire have been bound
together over an upside-
down bowl to form a cage
which has been placed over
a massed dome of vintage
Rosa 'Cool Water' in a low
bowl.

left It is easy to create a contemporary look by covering plastic orchid tubes with a strong long-lasting leaf such as ivy or *Galax* and inserting a single flower such as *Anthurium*, *Gerbera* or rose. The tube is then bound to a strong support: for example, a branch with decorative wire, bind wire or cable ties. If you find it hard to insert the stem make a nick in the plastic top, by the opening.

right In this design, decorative aluminium wire has been manipulated in the hands to create a structure to which pearl beads have been attached. The *Vanda* orchids have been inserted into small tubes pushed through the wire so they are hidden.

below Vintage is very much the trend. In this design sprigs of mature *Hydrangea* have been bound together with wire to create a garland at the base of the round glass bowl. The *Hydrangea* will dry in situ. The base of a foam sphere has been removed so that the sphere stands firm. This has been covered with a mass of *Rosa* 'La Belle' – a lovely vintage rose that blends beautifully with the soft tones of the *Hydrangea*.

right The china, table covering and accessories are all fashionably vintage. Tulips, in a cheerful assortment of colours, fill the cups to give easy flow along the table.

Techniques

Here are some of the terms used in contemporary design.

Bunching

Bunching is an expression used when many stems of the same flower are placed parallel to each other to form one unit. The stems can then be left free in position, or tied with raffia or another material that will blend. The tie should be of secondary interest. The stems can be approximately the same height or step down in height.

Bundling

Bundling is another term that is used to describe the mass positioning of one variety of flower in a parallel format. The difference is that the tie is of decorative interest and is an integral part of the design.

Groundwork/patchwork/tuft work/carpeting/pavé

These terms are all used to describe the method of covering the base of a design with very short stems of plant material of varying forms, colours and textures. One type of plant material leads into another and distinguishes itself by virtue of strong contrast. There can be some variation in height.

Grouping

Grouping is used in both contemporary and classic design to give a modern edge. It is exciting and challenging.

Flowers, foliage, berries and seedheads are grouped, not scattered. There is usually only one group placement of each variety. The important criterion is balance. Each time a placement is made it must be balanced by another placement, although its colour, form and texture are unlikely to be the same.

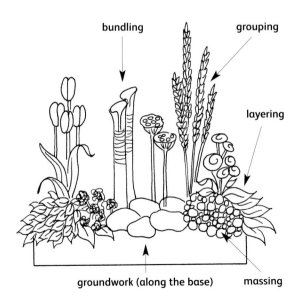

bundling — grouping — layering — groundwork (along the base) — massing

below In this grouped tapestry design the strong line of *Rosa* 'Cherry Brandy' and *Leucospermum* is balanced to the left with the dark *Heuchera* leaves and baubles and to the right with decorative metallic wire, ribbon and space.

Layering or terracing

A way of understanding layering is to think of tiles on a roof. Layering is the placing of several different types of leaf, or many of the same, on top of each other. They can be angled slightly to give depth and movement.

above and right In this design by Stef Adriaenssens, he uses the layering technique to create a foliage column offering an extended container for some perfect oriental lilies.

Massing or blocking

Immediate impact can be created by massing together plant material of one flower or leaf type. Individual form does not exist, only the mass as a whole. Space may occur by cutting stems to different lengths so that the heads are at different heights within the mass to avoid flatness.

right *Dianthus* (carnations) have an unhappy reputation of being boring – an opinion with which I strongly disagree. Carnation heads, as a mass, offer glorious colour and texture. Here about 20 carnations are massed together, with no space between the stems, and placed in a glass cube lined with variegated *Aspidistra*. A stack of four manipulated plain *Aspidistra* is inserted alongside to give contrast and balance.

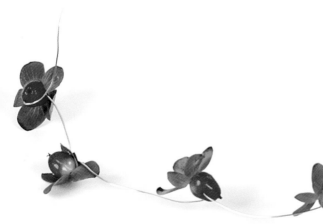

Threading

Threading is an easy but effective technique where plant material is threaded on to bullion/decorative wire, strong cotton or fishing line to create a long length of plant material. Multiple strings can create a floral curtain. Long-lasting carnations and *Cymbidium* or *Phalaenopsis* orchids work well.

below A design by Stef Adriaenssens. Here he has suspended a mass of glass tubes from a huge structure, each containing the head of a *Phalaenopsis* orchid.

below Fishing wire is threaded through the heads of *Chrysanthemum* 'Anastasia', pearl beads and roses to create a stunning floral curtain.

Leaf manipulation

Taking a leaf and changing its form is possible with tough, long-lasting plant material such as *Aspidistra, Bergenia, Fatsia* (Japanese aralia), *Galex, Hedera* (ivy), palms and *Phormium* (New Zealand flax). The following are some of the techniques commonly practised.

Angling

Perhaps the plant material that lends itself most to creating graphic line forms is the *Equisetum* (horsetail). Its straight form is easily manipulated at angles, thus giving enclosed space within an arrangement. Bamboo can also be cut to length and fixed together with wire or electricians' cable ties to give angled shapes.

below A design on a posy pad using *Brassica* (ornamental cabbages), *Hydrangea*, mini *Gerbera* and roses. The angled reeds used here are not hollow but still incorporate stems into the design and add interest.

Folding

Take any long-lasting, glossy green leaf, such as large ivy or laurel leaves, and fold once, twice or even three times to get the shape you want. Overlap them until you have acquired the desired effect.

right Repetition gives interest and holds the eye. Here the multiple folded leaves create a backcloth against which any flowers would look stunning.

Looping

Loop the tip of the leaf down to meet the top of the stem. Staple, bind with tape or position a blob of florists' fix where the two parts of the leaf meet.

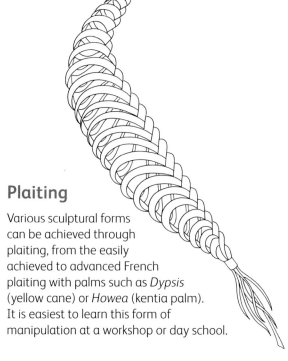

Piercing

Hold an *Aspidistra* so that you are facing the back. Bend the stem up and poke the stem end through the centre of the leaf, close to the main rib, and pull down.

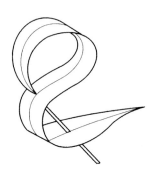

Plaiting

Various sculptural forms can be achieved through plaiting, from the easily achieved to advanced French plaiting with palms such as *Dypsis* (yellow cane) or *Howea* (kentia palm). It is easiest to learn this form of manipulation at a workshop or day school.

below An *Aspidistra* leaf has been pierced in a simple technique that is always effective.

below A basic plaiting technique with flexi grass can produce an interesting effect.

Rolling

Take a *Galax* or *Bergenia* leaf and roll it into a cone shape. Secure with staples or dressmaking or pearl-headed pins.

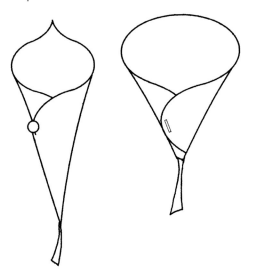

below Any round, strong leaf such as ivy or *Galax* can be rolled into a cup shape.

Stapling

This method of plant manipulation is ideal for small *Rhapis* (miniature fan palms). Their tips are stapled together in pairs (if there are three left at the end, staple them together). The tips are then bent over and taped to the top of the stem.

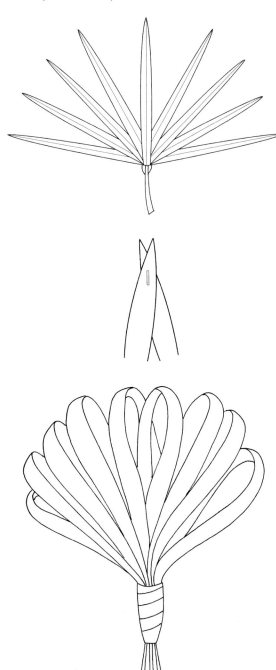

Weaving

Divide a leaf such as *Phormium* into six strips lengthways or use a bunch of the simple strap leaves of China grass or lily grass. Weave the first strip over the second, then under the third and so on until the strip is on the opposite side to where you started. Repeat with the other strips until one is left. Turn the work over and repeat until one is left.

Winding or wrapping

Low glass bowls are ideal for showing leaves wrapped round and round upon themselves to create a circular rather than a linear form. Ideal leaves are those that are flexible, long-lasting and linear, such as *Aspidistra, Cordyline* or *Phormium*.

top left Decorative wire has been woven over and under strands of bear grass.

left *Typha* has been woven to create a surround for an unexciting plastic container.

above *Phormium* leaves, which grow prolifically in the garden, have been wrapped around the inside of a low glass bowl. The circles of leaves support the roses and berries and need no further mechanic.

Wiring

Place wire along the central length of a strong, dry leaf and secure with florists' tape. Start 5 cm (2 in) from the tip as this is the most transparent part of the leaf and the wire may be seen through. Manipulate by coiling or bending to give an undulating form.

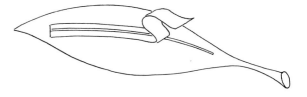

Structures/constructions

Structures, also known as constructions, are often made from fresh or dried plant material frequently with twigs or trailing stems, which are secured by tying, nailing, threading, weaving, winding, wedging or bending.

Structures may be used in place of ordinary mechanics. They can be added to give decorative as well as supportive value.

The plant material used for making structures may be:

- trailing, such as climbers: *Clematis*, *Hedera* (ivy), *Jasminum* (jasmine) and *Parthenocissus tricuspidata* (Boston ivy)
- weeping: *Betula* (birch) and *Salix* (willow)
- stems or twigs of a woody nature: *Eucalyptus*, *Kerria*, roses or stripped *Salix* (willow).

Lengths of trailing or weeping plant material can be wound or tied together at random or fixed in definite patterns to give rings or spheres. Woody stems are ideal for creating grids and other more graphic forms.

below A simple grid of *Cornus* (dogwood) supports nine rose heads stripped of their leaves. The grid has been created using OASIS® Bindwire.

Flexible stems such as willow withies or *Cornus* (dogwood) can be manipulated to form curving structures. These make perfect frameworks for handtied arrangements, or hanging glass test tubes holding flowers.

above Believe it or not the base of this design is potatoes. A structure of flexible stems has been manipulated to follow the form of the floating ring. Covered plastic cones, inserted through the structure, support stems of *Gloriosa superba* 'Rothschildiana'.

right Mikado sticks have been bound together irregularly to create a structure on a handmade container of 'iron' wires and bindwire. Sea horse glass tubes have been attached to the structure into which the flower stems of *Clematis*, *Gloriosa superba* 'Rothschildiana' and *Vanda* orchids have been inserted.

right In this design, by one of my favourite German designers, Felix Geiling-Rasmus, *Brassica napus* (rape seed) stems have been inverted so the roots are uppermost to provide a structure for the support of the fresh flower stems.

Spheres

Spheres, in a line or grouped, can provide an innovative centrepiece for the table or be used on a large scale for contemporary design work.

Suitable plant material for dry foam spheres

- individual leaves of *Eucalyptus*
- flat moss
- reindeer moss
- glycerined leaves
- *Galax* leaves
- *Brachyglottis* syn. *Senecio* leaves
- cloves
- dried lichen
- dried seeds and beans
- dried seedheads
- squares/pieces of birch bark

Suitable plant material for wet foam balls

- carnations
- spray carnations
- spray chrysanthemums
- ivy leaves
- sections of *Aspidistra* or *Phormium* leaves
- *Galax* leaves
- *Craspedia*
- *Sedum*
- *Viburnum tinus*
- *Hedera arborescens* (berried ivy)
- *Hydrangea*

left Here spheres of *Chrysanthemum* 'Kermit' line the steps at a flower festival at Chicheley Hall.

Making a sphere

You will need

- sphere or square of foam
- pearl-headed pins, brass tacks, steel pins or glue
- plant material (see page 220).

Method

1 If making your own bespoke sphere rub your square of foam in your hands so that it becomes the required size.

2 If you wish to wet the sphere, allow it to sink under its own weight in deep water. This will take about 30 seconds. You can remove a sliver of foam so that it will rest more securely on a plate or low dish.

3 Pin, glue or insert your plant material.

above Lime-green spheres are teamed with tea lights for a dramatic contemporary table centre. The individual heads of *Chrysanthemum* 'Santini' are ideal for making spheres. Do be careful if placing on the table directly unless you cover the base with plastic film.

Tapestry design

The beauty of the tapestry or pavé design lies in the massed contrasts of adjacent texture, form and colour. Plump berries can lie next to prickly teasels, fluffy seedheads close to smooth leaves. Layering is often a feature. Follow these guidelines for creating a simple tapestry.

Guidelines

- You can include organic and non-organic decorations.
- Group your components to give impact.
- Try to build pathways for the eye to follow through the design.
- Although this is a low arrangement, the height of the plant material can be varied to give interest.
- Use bun, flat, reindeer or *Tillandsia* (Spanish moss) and sisal to help cover the foam surface and reduce cost. Pin in place.
- Enclosed space can be created with bridging material or loops of grasses or grass-like materials.
- Design can be formal or more informal.
- Foam is often used as the mechanic.
- Decorative detailing can include beads, coloured wire, stones, shells, wool and fabric – even pan scourers!

right A rich tapestry of colour, form and texture designed by Laura Leong, with the purple *Vanda* orchids and *Clematis* flowers holding centre stage. *Celosia argentea* var. *cristata* and *Viburnum lantana* berries add colour and texture and mini gourds and assorted exotic fruits (the round forms that look like sea urchins and giant gooseberries) create additional interest.

below A low bowl holds a tapestry of *Alchemilla mollis*, *Allium*, *Heuchera* leaves, *Hydrangea*, *Paeonia* (peony) and its foliage. *Dahlia* provide a pathway through the design for the eye to follow.

Embroidered tapestry

Textured, embroidered tapestry designs were seen in Germany in the early 2000s. Unlike the tapestry design shown in the step by step (see pages 226–7), embroidered tapestries use small-scale plant material and are intricate and detailed, with the plant material scattered or used to form patterns. Floral foam is used as the base for stronger-stemmed plant material. I like to use a criss-cross of tape through which stems can be threaded directly into water, which is ideal for all plant material. Suitable plant material could be *Alchemilla mollis*, *Astrantia*, *Bouvardia*, *Bupleurum*, spray *Chrysanthemum*, *Hypericum* berries, *Matricaria*, *Ornithogalum* (chincherinchee), *Viola*, spray roses, daisies from the garden and even buttercups!

right In the summer, stems have strengthened and can be easily inserted in foam, which is placed slightly lower than the rim of the container. *Fatsia japonica* produces seedheads similar to those of the tree ivy but they have a lovely white colour and strong stems. Here they have been used with *Eryngium* (sea holly), *Eustoma* (lisianthus), white *Trachelium* and *Senecio maritima* foliage.

right A turquoise bowl is
packed with groups of
vibrant orange *Ranunculus*,
roses and *Leucospermum* to
give a striking design of
complementary colours.

Tapestry design in a low bowl

You will need

- low bowl filled with foam to just below the rim or a posy pad in the size of your choice
- 5–10 different groups of decoration
- 3–4 stems of flexi grass (optional).

Method

1 Wet the foam and secure in the bowl. Alternatively wet the posy pad. Place it horizontally on water that is deep enough to submerge it fully. It will take about 60 seconds to soak.

2 Start to group your plant material. Each group should be placed adjacent to another and contrast in form and texture.

3 You can create a larger design by extending the outline with more linear plant material.

4 Add leaves, fruit, seedheads or berries with a smooth, plain texture to give calm relief.

5 Create interest by subtly varying the height of the individual elements within each group.

6 Layer some of the plant material.

7 Before inserting the *Hypericum* remove a few berries from the bottom. Thread these berries on to the flexi grass. This is easier to do than you may think but if you push a wire through the berry first it will be even easier.

8 Create enclosed space by tucking the two ends of each stem of flexi grass into the foam. Avoid making the loops too large or they will upset the overall balance of the design.

Parallel design

The parallel design is also known as a landscape design. As the dominant direction can be portrait (vertical) as well as landscape (horizontal) I feel the term 'parallel' is a more apt description.

This style of design came into being some decades ago and originated in Holland. The first styles were rather regimented, with a strong vertical movement and no gentle touch. It has been changed over the years to create a style that is still viewed as contemporary but has been modified to take account of the stem irregularity and imperfections of British garden plant material.

It can be created in a rectangular, circular or square container and the placements can be structured or more fluid, whichever way you prefer. Line, round or spray plant material can be used to create the vertical placements.

left A structured parallel design with three main vertical placements. In this particular design each component has been used only once and not scattered through the design.

right Here the elements are more relaxed but the overall movement of the design is vertical and upward.

below This is a design I loved doing, using roses, spray roses, spray *Chrysanthemum* 'Green Lizard' and *Leucospermum* on a bed of tree ivy. Shiny baubles give a festive feel. It was incredibly easy and quick to create. Placing trays together gives horizontal as well as vertical movement.

Here I give a method for a more structured design with a horizontal, landscape emphasis. For information on techniques used in parallel designs refer to page 204.

A structured parallel design

You will need

- low tray and floral foam or a mini/medi OASIS® Deco
- mix of linear and round flowers such as *Allium*, *Delphinium*, small sunflowers and *Liatris* that can be staggered in height to give an overall vertical movement
- round flowers if your vertical placements are linear rather than round to give focus at the base
- short stems of foliage for the groundwork
- smooth-textured leaves for the groundwork
- berries, stones, cones, fruit and/or vegetables, moss or sisal (optional)

Method

1 Soak the foam (see page 44) and place in the container or use the OASIS® Deco. The foam should be higher than the container so that you can layer plant material out of the sides.

2 Create your vertical placements. For a container about 25 cm (10 in) long three verticals look good. If longer use four or more – there is no limit. Position the outer placements slightly in from the ends to ensure good balance. The verticals can be bunched or bound or simply graduated down in height. Most stems will have their own point of origin and will not radiate from a central core, although radiation does frequently exist to create a less rigid design.

3 If your verticals are of linear plant material rather than round, you may want to add some round flowers at the base to give focal dominance. Keep them low and relatively central as the strength of their form could otherwise upset the overall balance of the design.

4 Cover your foam with short plant material. Keep it in blocks of contrasting form, texture and colour. Do include smooth-textured plant material such as *Aspidistra*, ivy and *Fatsia*. Clip or manipulate them to fit the space and add interest.

5 You may wish to add flowers such as spray chrysanthemums or *Limonium* (statice) that can be broken down into short units to bring colour to the base of the design. Alternatively you could add fruit and vegetables, stones or moss to give interest and cut down on cost!

6 Areas/blocks of uncluttered material provide 'rest' within a design and contrast with busy bundles or layered groundwork.

Variation

You could use a round container or basket and create a close structure with grasses or reeds. The flowers are simply graduated through the structure.

right In a square container with a bed of dried *Hydrangea* and Christmas baubles, stems of red and green *Cornus* take the eye upwards, strengthened by the addition of red roses.

Spirals

Spirals are often created from bear grass, flexi grass or steel grass as they can be easily manipulated into circular forms and last well out of water. Decorative reel wire can be used to hold the spiral in shape.

Wired bear grass spiral

This spiral takes one bunch of bear grass and a reel of decorative wire. It is easier to create than it sounds. It can support one large or a few smaller flowers and will last for weeks.

You will need

- bunch of bear grass
- 1 elastic band
- 1 roll of decorative reel wire
- 3 *Zantedeschia*, 1 *Helianthus* (sunflower) or any other bold flowers.

Method

1 Place the elastic band tightly around the thick end of the stems, so that they cannot move.

2 Take a clump of about 12 adjacent pieces of grass. With the wire, bind these together by spiralling at equal distances about 10 times up the stems. Do not cut the wire.

3 Then take a clump of another six adjacent stems. Bend the first clump, so that it meets the new one. Secure with the wire by spiralling up the stems about six times.

4 Push the two secured clumps to one side, as far as they will go. This will create the round, spiral effect.

5 Take another clump of six stems, and secure to the previous clumps with the wire as before. Again, push them back as far as they will go.

6 The mass of clumps will now be getting longer and longer.

7 Repeat until there are only three or four strands of grass left in the middle. Now, spiral the wire to the very end of the stems.

8 Take the end as far around the circle as you can. Secure with the wire. Cut the wire.

9 Place the flower(s) in the centre of the spiral.

right The finished spiral holds three stems of *Zantedeschia* (calla lilies).

Popular themes

Some contemporary floral designs can be inspired by current 'hot' trends from the world of popular culture.

Cupcakes

In US television series *Sex and the City* viewers saw the character Carrie Bradshaw (played by Sarah Jessica Parker) devouring an exquisitely iced cupcake in the Magnolia Bakery, New York. From that point on it was cool to eat cake, and cupcakes in particular!

Making cupcakes is a satisfying and creative way of working with plant material. Group a selection together or arrange on a cake stand as an innovative table centrepiece. I made a selection of cupcakes for Alan Titchmarsh and Jo Swift at a television broadcast for Chelsea Flower Show and they loved them.

Floral cupcakes

You will need

- **cupcake holders**
- **piece of black plastic refuse bag**
- **hairpins of wire**
- **foam of a size to suit**
- **plant material to cover such as:**
  - Santini *Chrysanthemum* (which are very small)
  - small *Eryngium* (sea holly)
  - *Hypericum* berries
  - *Gypsophila*
  - star anise
  - cloves
  - pieces of cinnamon sticks.

Method

1 Take a foam sphere and cut it in two. To make your own sphere or half-sphere from a piece of foam, cut a square from a brick of foam and rub with the hands to produce a cake of the required size. Soak briefly or spray with water.

2 Cover the flat base with a piece of black plastic. Secure with hairpins of wire low down at the side.

3 Cut your small-scale plant material short and insert to create patterns or a mass.

Tip

Your cupcakes will last longer if you use cases made from silicone rather than paper. Paper cases tend to flatten quickly when in close proximity to wet foam. Silicone cases are easily available from specialist shops and online.

left An eclectic assortment of cupcakes in paper cases topped by a cake created on a small posy pad base bound with decorative ribbon.

right Cupcakes in plastic cases. Let your imagination have no bounds!

Handbags

Floral handbags are another fun and frivolous idea that is inexpensive to create. All you need is a piece of foam, a few long-lasting leaves and strands of flexi grass. Very popular as a floral theme for weddings and events, these handbags are lovely for the centre of a table to create an impact. If only lightly wetted they are perfect for a bridesmaid or for the catwalk.

Other suitable leaves would be:

- *Stachys lanata* (lamb's ears)
- *Hedera helix* (ivy)
- Hard ruscus
- *Galax*

below This handbag is covered with *Eucalyptus* leaves with a decorative buttonhole pinned to the front. Flexi grass for the 'handle' is ideal as it is smooth-textured. Bear grass or spear grass may cut the hand. Do not hold by the handle when the foam is wet – see tip on the opposite page.

Floral handbags

You will need

- **half brick of foam**
- **piece of black plastic refuse sack or cellophane**
- **florists' pins**
- **several strands of *Ficinia* (flexi grass)**
- **medium gauge florists' wire**
- **decorative wire**
- **long-lasting, evenly shaped leaves such as *Eucalyptus cineria* or hard ruscus**
- **flowers of choice.**

Method

1 With a sharp knife cut the foam into a handbag shape. Keep the base about 7.5 cm (3 in) wide at the bottom, 2.5 cm (1 in) at the top and about 10 cm (4 in) tall.

2 Take two or three strands of flexi grass. Wire each end with a long single legged mount by bending a medium-gauge florists' wire so that one end is longer than the other. Place on the stem towards the end and wrap the longer wire around the stem and the shorter end three times. The free ends should be straight and parallel to one another. Push both ends through the top of the foam so they protrude out of the bottom. Turn the excess wire back into the foam.

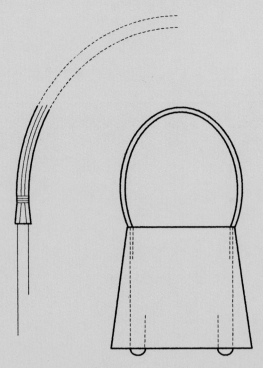

below This handbag is made from hard ruscus leaves with a decoration of plant material along the top.

3 Embellish and strengthen the flexi grass with decorative wire if so desired.

4 Spray the foam lightly with water.

5 Cut a piece of refuse sack or cellophane to cover the base and to come approximately one-third of the way up the sides. Pin in place.

6 Cover the top of the foam with overlapping leaves. Work down the bag from the top. The tip of the leaves should stand slightly higher than the top of the foam if you want flowers at the top. Keep a neat regular pattern with the pins. At the bottom tuck any excess leaf under the bag and pin in place.

7 Spray the bag with water or Chrysal Glory® (see page 40).

8 Gently push a few well-conditioned robust flowers through the uncovered area at the top of the foam. You can make a slit in the leaves to make insertion easier. Alternatively make a simple buttonhole and pin it securely to the foam.

Tip

If you soak the whole piece of foam it would be very heavy and the handle would not be secure. Just dip the tip of the foam in water if you wish to position flowers only along the top of the handbag.

CHAPTER 6 · CONTEMPORARY DESIGN **239**

*O*ften family and friends will come together to create one of the most important elements of a wedding – the flowers. Flowers give a sense of joy, beauty and celebration. Whether classic, vintage or contemporary, flowers at the ceremony and reception complete the picture.

Most brides have flowers they particularly love, often sweet-smelling flowers such as peonies, *Freesia*, lily-of-the-valley or sweet peas. Colour is usually of great importance, as are budget and style.

CHAPTER 7
WEDDING FLOWERS

For amateurs creating flower arrangements for such an important event can be quite a daunting task. Some of the step by step designs that I have outlined in previous chapters are ideal for the marriage ceremony and civil reception.

Perhaps the most relevant are:

Round table design, page 158
- Table centres at the reception.
- On the table for the signing of the register.
- For the entrance table of the church or reception.

Long and low table design, page 164
- For the top table.
- On the church altar (if this is allowed).

Mantelpiece design, page 167
- On window ledges in the church or at the reception.
- For the top of a mantelpiece in the reception area.

Tall table design, page 170
- For the front-facing top table for the bridal party.

Pedestal design, page 180
- Either side of the table or altar for the ceremony.
- To the side of the wedding party as the guests are greeted.
- Wherever a large design on a stable base is required.

Ring design, page 193
- At the base of a candelabra or with a thick candle for the table centres at the reception.

Parallel design, page 232
- At the foot of the altar, choir stalls or any other focal structure.
- On window ledges at the ceremony or reception.
- Along the centre of a reception table as long as it is not too high.

right The colours of summer glow in this exuberant all-round design in a fibreglass urn.

left Blues and purples are very popular colours for wedding flowers. Just make sure that the lighting is sufficiently good so that these recessive colours do not disappear and become dark holes. There were two pedestal designs, one each side of the bride and groom, facing the guests in a large open room at Burleigh House. Hydrangeas are brilliant at bringing large scale flowers into a big design, at a reasonable cost, during late summer and the autumn.

THE WEDDING CEREMONY AND RECEPTION

If time and budget are limited I would argue that the most important single design for the ceremony is the pedestal or urn of flowers facing the couple. Everyone is looking at this arrangement. It is far better to have one splendid design in a noticeable position than many smaller pieces scattered around. In some venues it is possible to move the pedestal to the reception but only do this if you must. By the time it has been lifted, transported, repositioned and the pollen from the lilies has left a splendid trail down the best man's shirt and the whole thing looks a damaged mess, you will begin to agree with me!

below *Eustoma* (lisianthus), *Lathyrus* (sweet pea) and *Dianthus* (carnation) are massed individually to provide a block of texture and form united by the colour white. For a reception table for ten, the three arrangements on the mirrored glass would be great. For a smaller table the arrangements could be used singly.

Wedding favours

Wedding favours are a long-standing and traditional way of thanking your guests for coming to share in your special day.

The most traditional wedding favour, originating from Italy, is a box or bag containing five sugared almonds, representing health, wealth, happiness, fertility and a long life. However, in recent years many people have broken with this tradition and gifts now range from handmade chocolates to toiletries and even to lottery tickets!

Floral gifts for guests to take away are very popular and they can fit in with the overall theme of the wedding.

right Wrap a length of double sided tape around an empty yoghurt pot and stick on long-lasting bay leaves. Tie with raffia. Place flowers of your choice in your container. Here I have used *Viburnum* blossom/flowers and one stem of spray roses.

Single rose favour

Since opening my flower school this simple design has proved more popular than any other. It is long-lasting, can be made in minutes well in advance of the wedding and is the perfect name card or memento to be taken away by the guests as an alternative to sugared almonds.

Method

1 Wet the foam by placing the rectangle on the top of water that is deeper than the foam. Allow the foam to sink until level with the water (about 10 seconds) and the colour of the foam has changed from mid to dark green.

2 Place the square of plastic sheet on the base of the foam. Fold the plastic around the base of the foam. Bend short lengths from the stub wire and insert in the sides of the plastic to secure. This will avoid any possible water damage.

You will need

- rectangle of foam (you can make 16 rectangles from one standard brick of foam) approximately 7.5 cm (3 in) tall and 2.5 cm (1 in) square
- square of black plastic sheet cut from a refuse sack (one bag produces hundreds)
- 1 medium-gauge stub wire
- 1 *Aspidistra* leaf
- pearl-headed pin
- 2–3 round ivy or *Galax* leaves
- 1 rose
- gold or silver pen to personalise the design.

3 Take the *Aspidistra* leaf. Feel the leaf and remove the stalk and the part of the leaf which is semi-rigid. You should leave sufficient leaf to wrap round the foam at least one and a half times.

4 Look at your leaf. One side has a greater curve than the other. Hold the straighter side level with the base of the foam covered with plastic and wrap tightly around the foam. Pin the tip of the *Aspidistra* leaf to the foam. If the leaf rises high above the top of the foam, cut it so that it is level or slightly higher than the foam. You have now created your container.

5 Take two or three ivy or *Galax* leaves. Cut the stems to about 2.5 cm (1 in) and insert into the foam so that the stems radiate from the centre of the foam.

6 Cut the rose short, about 5 cm (2 in), and place centrally.

7 To personalise, write the name of the guest on one of the leaves with a gold or silver pen.

above A single rose wedding favour using a head of *Rosa* 'Grand Prix'.

above For this favour, bay leaves have been pinned on to a piece of wet foam which has its base covered in thin film to avoid water damage. Start at the top of the foam and work downwards with your leaves. A couple of *Dianthus* (carnations) have been inserted in the top of the foam.

Hanging designs

This design is often used on the backs of chairs or hanging from church pews, walls, doors or pillars. It could also double as a table arrangement at the reception if the handle is well hidden with flowers and foliage.

The mechanics for hanging arrangements are inexpensive, and the plant material can be limited yet effective. There are also spray trays available that have a plastic cage over a piece of foam. These are quick and easy to use but cost considerably more than the basic spray tray. The result is just the same, although the larger caged tray allows for a larger design with added support.

Ideally hanging designs should be arranged in situ to ensure that the design is well balanced and attractive from all sides, but they can be made in advance.

The hanging design can be shield-shaped, as described in the step by step on the following page, or have the stems showing as part of the design.

right Yellow mini *Gerbera*, blue *Eryngium* (sea holly), x *Solidaster* and dainty nodding *Matricaria*, which has amazingly strong stems and long-lasting flowers, are arranged in a tray with a handle. The discarded stalks are added separately to give the effect of a bouquet of flowers.

Hanging design or pew end

You will need

- OASIS® Spray Tray with handle or a caged pew end (see page 54)
- ¼–⅓ brick of foam
- florists' tape
- outline foliage such as *Danae racemosa* (hard ruscus), *Eucalyptus*, *Gaultheria* (salal tips) or *Ligustrum* (privet)
- round flowers such as 5 mini *Gerbera* or roses
- spray flowers such as *Hypericum*, *Anigozanthos* (kangaroo paw), *Alchemilla mollis* or *Solidago* (golden rod)
- filler foliage such as *Pittosporum*.

Method

1 Cut the foam to fit the tray tightly. The foam should rise approximately twice as high as the container's depth. If you are preparing the pew end in situ, water may drip on the floor when inserting your stems. To avoid this, either cover the foam with cling-film or wet the foam 24 hours in advance and allow it to dry out a little. If covering with cling film, ensure that the tape securing it is at the bottom of the tray as more than one layer of film makes it harder to penetrate.

2 Strap the foam firmly in place with florists' tape. One length of tape, overlapping at the base, should be sufficient.

3 If hanging on a pew end, suspend by threading ribbon or paper-covered wire through the hanging hole and tying around the sides of the pew end. An alternative means of suspension would be to thread a wire hook through the hole and then hooking it over the top. If hanging on a wall you could hang the spray tray on a nail or screw. Alternatively use ribbon or wire as for the pew end.

4 Create the depth of the design. If the aisle is narrow you will not want it to extend too much. The first stem should be placed in the centre of the foam, **a**. The second stem should be at right angles to the first stem and cover the spray tray's handle, **b**. The third stem should extend downwards to make a design of the desired size, **c**.

5 You now need to create an oval design by placing:

- short stems horizontally out of the two sides, **d**
- longer stems radiating from the central area of the foam, **e**

- further stems out of the top of the foam so that they radiate from the central area, **X**, of the foam, **f**. These stems should not be too long or the wall hanging will lose its shape.

6 Create a stronger form by adding more outline foliage within the form created.

7 Add your round flowers. Ensure that you have colour and flowers at the sides of the design and not just full on as the pews will be viewed from the side as people walk up and down the aisle.

8 Insert the filler flowers through the design.

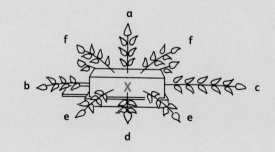

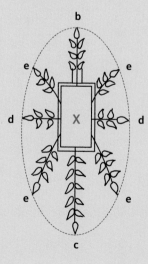

Decorating the top of a pillar or post

Take a length of strong fishing line or strong reel wire around the top of the ridge on a pillar. Using further lengths of wire, thread each through the hole in the spray tray containing foam. Hang them at intervals to that they lie flat against the wire around the pillar. Make sure they are secure and not likely to fall.

Angle foliage out of the foam so that a circle of plant material is created around the column and the trays are hidden. Add long-lasting flowers to give interest.

This method can also be used around a square pillar.

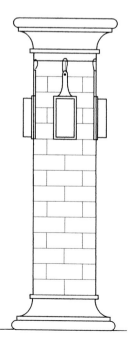

below Bridal *Gladiolus*, spider *Chrysanthemum*, green *Anthurium and Dianthus* (carnations) go further with the addition of variegated foliage. Here, cream *Euonymus* adds interest and variety to the pillar surround at Chicheley Hall.

Giant topiary

A giant topiary is a tall, striking design that is so easy to make once you have the mechanics in place. It is also inexpensive, yet looks very impressive. A pair of topiaries is ideal outdoors to flank the entrance to a building.

Topiary design

To create effective topiary designs you need to select bold, robust flowers, especially if they are to stand outside. In this design spray chrysanthemums come into their own and I particularly love the single white. If on a budget the wild *Leucanthemum vulgare* (ox-eye daisies) work just as well. For big impact and lovely colours use hydrangeas, but only in late summer and the autumn, when the blooms are strong and unlikely to wilt.

You will need

- plastic bucket
- quick-drying cement or plaster of Paris
- stones or pieces of broken terracotta pot to give ballast
- birch pole or broom handle about 1 m (3 ft 3 in) long
- thick rubber band
- decorative outer container for your bucket
- square of floral foam rounded by rubbing with the hands. You could also use a foam sphere, but this is much more expensive and no more effective
- mixed foliage
- flowers – I nearly always use spray chrysanthemums
- berries or seedheads (optional)
- ribbon (optional).

Method

1 Place a few stones at the bottom of the bucket, leaving a hole at the centre for the pole. Follow the instructions on the packet to mix the quick-drying cement or plaster of Paris with water. Pour the mix into the bucket so that it is half full. Hold the pole in place until the cement or plaster has started to set.

2 Once it has set, take a strong rubber band over the top of the pole and down 5 cm (2 in). This will stop your foam sliding down the pole. Place the bucket in a more decorative outer container.

3 Wet the foam and insert on top of the pole. Push down firmly until it meets the band and is wedged on the top.

4 Using foliage that is relatively linear, aim to create a ball of foliage and flowers that is equal in volume to that of the outer container. The first stem should be placed vertically out of the top of the foam and the second vertically downwards.

5 Four stems should be placed horizontally out of the sides of the foam. Be sure you do not place them at an angle. They should be equidistant from each other.

6 Fill in the 'ball' by adding more stems. Angle all the stems from the central area **X** in order to create a sphere.

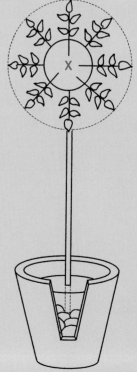

7 Add your spray chrysanthemums. There is no better flower than this for outdoor topiary. They are long-lasting, robust and have the extra advantage of being inexpensive and totally beautiful when you do not see the stems.

8 If necessary add more foliage to fill the shape. Variegated foliage (those of two colours such as white and green) will fill the design and give the impression of flowers when viewed from a distance.

right Beautiful blue hydrangeas are mixed with the pink spray chrysanthemums on a base of *Gaultheria* (salal tips). Green *Eustoma* (lisianthus) lighten the picture.

Large design in an urn

Large arrangements in urns are becoming more and more popular for both the ceremony and the reception. They are designed so that they can be viewed from three sides (when placed close to a wall) or in the round (for the centre of a room). Here I describe how to make one to be seen in the round, to distinguish it from the more classic three-sided pedestal design on page 180.

right A luxurious green foliage background supports roses, *Hydrangea*, *Eustoma* (lisianthus) and spray roses. The flowers are grouped to give greater impact in these wonderful urn designs by Robbie Honey.

Urn design

You will need

- **plinth and urn**
- **bucket to fit inside the urn**
- **OASIS® Floral Foam Jumbo Foam Brick(s)**
- **linear foliage and flowers such as *Eucalyptus* and *Antirrhinum***
- **smooth-textured leaves such as *Hosta***
- **round flowers such as *Hydrangea* and roses**
- **spray flowers such as spray roses**
- **additional foliage (optional).**

Method

1 Insert the soaked foam in the bucket. The bucket will be placed in the urn so check that the foam rises well above the rim of the urn. If not raise the bucket on bricks of old foam.

2 Insert stem **a** of linear plant material in the centre of the foam. This stem will establish the finished size of the design. To get good proportions make it approximately the same height as the urn and the foam (without the plinth).

3 The majority of stems **b** are the same length as **a**. Some will be shorter to give interesting variation. These will be positioned in all directions out of the foam, but every stem will appear to radiate from area **X** in the centre of the visible foam. You need to position the stems so that there is a uniform distance between them. Angle stems downwards over the rim of the container.

4 Help to cover the foam and to give a contrast of texture by placing large leaves, with a smooth texture, through the design. Let the stems have movement, so do not cut them too short. They should not go beyond the boundaries set by the linear material. At this point the foam will be visible but not dominant. If you feel too much foam is showing add more outline linear foliage.

5 Take linear flowers through the design. Place the first stem dead centre as this will help establish symmetry. The flowers along the stems will fill the design with colour at all levels. Keep the flowers within the shape created by the foliage.

6 Add round flowers through the design. The stems should be approximately the same length and placed at angles to give interest. The stems will be slightly shorter than the foliage framework.

7 Complete with sprays of berries or flowers or perhaps some interesting foliage. You could add fruits such as lemons, apples or kiwi fruit, or vegetables such as shallots or broccoli. These can be impaled on lengths of garden wire or kebab sticks. Do remember, though, that ripe fruit can shorten the life of the design as it gives off ethylene gas.

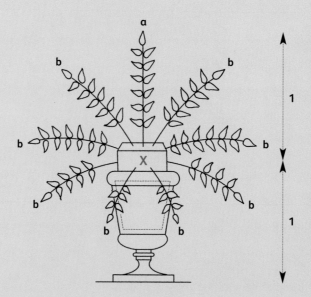

right From mid-summer to late autumn there is no better flower than the *Hydrangea* to create a stunning design in an urn. Seven to nine heads create an impressive display. Although expensive to buy they are easy to grow in most gardens. Their scale reduces the need to purchase as many smaller-scale flowers.

Candelabra

Paying for decorated candelabras can cost a fortune. If you have space the best option is to purchase a basic candelabra and decorate it yourself. Flat moss and trailing ivy create a wonderful effect inexpensively and if you have the budget you can easily create a central placement of flowers.

There are plenty of candelabras available but I would suggest you use those that are at least 1 m (3 ft 3 in) high. The method on the following page is for a candelabra that has seen better days! A pristine silver one is best left in all its glory.

right Foam has been placed on the central dish integral to this candelabra. Trails of garden ivy cascade to the floor while the top is packed with beautiful *Rosa* 'Avalanche', *Eryngium* (sea holly) and *Trachelium*.

Moss-covered candelabra

To cover the candelabra you will need

- **tray of flat moss**
- **reel of wire**
- **trails of ivy**
- **petals for scattering at the base** (optional).

Method

1 Holding the moss on the candelabra with one hand, wrap the wire over the moss and bind it in place.

2 Spray the moss with water and as an option insert the ends of well-conditioned trailing ivy in the moss and wrap around the candelabra.

3 Add your central placement of flowers in a similar way to that described on page 170 for a tall table design.

4 Scatter petals and/or add night lights and holders at the base if you so wish.

right A well-worn candlestick has been covered with moss and spiralled trails of ivy. The central placement is composed of soft ruscus, *Genista* (broom), *Eustoma* (lisianthus) and spray roses. A scattering of petals at the base completes the design.

THE BRIDAL PARTY

In this section, I outline designs for the bridal party that an enthusiastic amateur can create relatively easily. I have included a step by step for a simple wired buttonhole for those who would like to learn elementary wiring. It is best to leave the bridal flowers such as headdresses and wired bouquets to the professional florists as these are technically difficult. It would be dreadful if the flowers fell out of the home-made bouquet as the bride advanced up the aisle. A bridal bouquet of one type of flower is easy to create. However, the trend is moving towards the mixed bouquet to give variety and delight. It is more difficult to achieve a good balance of plant material, but a mixed bouquet does look lovely.

top left Three bridesmaid's bouquets incorporating vintage *Rosa* 'Amnesia', *Eustoma* (lisianthus), *Hydrangea*, herbs and snippets of garden foliage. This wedding was in the autumn – the ideal time to use the fashionable *Hydrangea*, which is now available in a broad spectrum of colours. In the spring and early summer *Hydrangea* is not reliable as a wedding flower as it is too early in the season.

left The bride's bouquet is similar to those of the bridesmaids but instead of the *Hydrangea* a wider selection of vintage roses has been used, together with larkspur and mint to give a special fragrance.

right The groom's buttonhole traditionally uses one of the flowers selected from the bride's bouquet. Here a perfect *Rosa* 'Amnesia' is framed with *Senecio cineraria* and the fruits of *Hedera arborescens* (tree ivy).

Pomander

A pomander is a charming decoration for a young bridesmaid, who will find it fun and easy to carry.

The sphere may be covered with leaves or flower heads. Using only one type of flower, such as a rose or single white *Chrysanthemum*, looks particularly effective. Small, flat flowers and dense, small-scale foliage such as *Asparagus umbellatus* (ming fern) or *Hebe* help to retain a spherical shape.

An alternative is a patchwork pomander in which different small-scale plant material is distributed around the sphere. Sweet-smelling herbs such as common myrtle (*Myrtus communis*) or short sprigs of rosemary would be particularly lovely. In season (from late summer to late autumn) florets of *Hydrangea* are invaluable.

A second alternative is a sphere covered with *Eucalyptus* leaves that will last well and can be made well in advance.

When making a pomander it is easier if you have access to a bouquet stand, from which the sphere can be hung while inserting the materials. A small-necked vase upon which the design can sit while you work would suffice.

Unlike the sphere on page 221 the pomander is carried by a ribbon loop. The finished design therefore needs to be as light as possible so the minimum amount of strain is put on the loop. A quick dip in water and a spray on completion should be sufficient to keep the plant material fresh for at least a day.

above Lime-green spray carnations form a simple and economical pomander.

Rose and foliage pomander

You will need

- 9 cm (3½ in) foam sphere – dry or wet
- 4–5 stems spray roses
- 1–2 stems ming fern
- snippets of *Hydrangea*, ming fern and/or rosemary
- 60 cm (2 ft) satin ribbon about 1.5 cm (¾ in) wide
- silver stub wire (0.46 mm)
- long 0.71 mm stub wire
- stem tape
- cold florists' glue.

Method

1 Dip the foam sphere for a few seconds in water. If the sphere is soaked thoroughly it will be too heavy and the handle will not be sufficiently secure.

2 Cut the ribbon to a length of approximately 25 cm (10 in) for the handle. Tightly wrap a strong silver wire (0.46 mm) round the ends of the ribbon. Leave two ends.

3 Join the ends of the wires together with stem tape. Now tape this to a sturdier, long 0.71 mm wire which will be strong enough to push through the foam sphere. A lighter wire would bend and be difficult to pass through the foam. Once it has appeared at the other end, return the remainder of the wire back into the foam. You can use a cross of florists' tape or a dab of cold glue over the insert and exit to give additional security.

4 If you wish to add a tail for the base of the pomander cut more ribbon to about 15 cm (6 in). Repeat the process used to make the handle in steps 2 and 3 and insert in the base.

5 Cut the rose stems short and insert in the foam at regular intervals. Fill in the gaps with short sprigs of *Hydrangea*, rosemary, ming fern or any other long-lasting flowers or foliage.

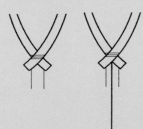

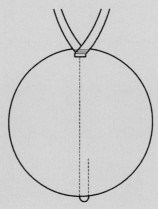

Method

1 Create a handle and tail as described in steps 2–4 on page 265.

2 Sort the leaves into uniform sizes. Leaves that are too big or too small will look visually uneven. Place the leaves on the work surface with the back facing upwards.

3 Dab a small amount of cold florists' glue all over the back of each leaf. Do eight leaves at a time and wait for about 30 seconds for the glue to go slightly tacky. This makes them stick more easily.

4 Starting at the handle, work out a preferred pattern for the leaves. Place the first leaf on the foam and press down gently until it has stuck firmly. Carry on sticking the other leaves to the foam, working in lines to achieve a neat pattern. Once one line is complete start the next line. Slightly overlap the leaves to avoid any gaps in the foam. Use pearl-headed pins to give extra security to the leaves and add decorative detail.

5 You can decorate the pomander by tucking a few spray roses into the top. Store in a cool place, but avoid misting directly on to the flowers or ribbon. Cover the pomander with tissue and spray the tissue lightly.

Tips

- Use *Eucalyptus* leaves from the florist as they will be more uniform than those picked from the garden (unless the foliage is juvenile).

- If you are using holly leaves use the variegated form with smooth margins.

Eucalyptus or holly pomander

You will need

- 9 cm (3½ in) dry foam sphere
- 60 cm (2 ft) satin ribbon about 1.5 cm (¾ in) wide
- silver stub wire (0.46 mm)
- long 0.71 mm stub wire
- stem tape
- cold florists' glue
- 30–50 *Eucalyptus cinerea* or holly leaves
- 1–2 stems spray roses (optional)
- pearl-headed pins.

Handtied wedding bouquet

A handtied wedding bouquet often uses a different technique to that described in Chapter 4 as the stems remain straight and the objective is to produce a rounded mass of flowers with little or no space between the flowers and foliage.

Perhaps the easiest handtied wedding bouquet is simply a mass of roses. The sturdiness of their stems means there is less risk of them breaking as you create your bouquet.

below Perfect peonies are always in fashion. Getting the peonies at the point of perfection is never easy. Buy more than you need, in tight bud, at least five days before the wedding and monitor their development.

above A mass of double *Freesia* on their own, and what could be lovelier?

right A mixed handtied bouquet of *Convallaria* (lily of the valley), roses, *Eryngium* (sea holly), *Eustoma* (lisianthus), *Freesia* and *Narcissus* with *Hebe* and a surround of *Galax* leaves.

above Unless you grow *Convallaria* (lily of the valley) in your garden they will always be expensive, even when in season. As the fragrance is irresistible, try incorporating their smooth-textured leaves to frame the flowers and create the perfect, dainty bouquet in April or May.

Rose handtied

A mass of beautiful cream roses, with a binding of satin ribbon, can easily create a bridal bouquet with or without a surround of leaves.

You will need

- 13–18 flat-headed roses such as *Rosa* 'Vendela' (cream) or *R.* 'Grand Prix' (red). The number used will depend on the size of the rose and the size of the desired bouquet.
- 20–30 large *Galax*, large ivy or *Parthenocissus tricuspidata* (Boston ivy) leaves
- florists' tape
- florists' wire – 0.28 mm or 0.32 mm (depending on the leaf's thickness and weight – the lighter the leaf the finer the wire)
- stem tape
- 1 m (3 ft 3 in) satin ribbon 2.5 cm (1 in) wide
- 3 pearl-headed pins.

Method

1 Remove all the leaves and thorns from the roses.

2 Mass the roses together in a gentle dome shape.

3 Wrap florists' tape firmly around the stems about 7 cm (2½ in) from the bottom of the flowers.

4 Wire the *Galax* or ivy leaves using the following method:

- cut the stem of the leaf so that it is about 2 cm (¾ in) long.
- hold the leaf between your finger and thumb with the underside of the leaf facing upwards.
- take a fine wire. Make a small stitch two-thirds of the way up the leaf, either side of the central vein.
- gently bring the two wires down parallel to the stem and wrap one around the stem and the other wire.

5 Tape the wires with stem tape, keeping it stretched so finely that it nearly snaps. If you are right-handed twirl the wire with your left hand and with your right pull the tape taut – away and down – at approximately a 130-degree angle. If left-handed perform this action in reverse.

6 Create two rings of wired leaves around the flowers. The first ring will have the back of the leaves outwards. The second ring will have the front of the leaves outwards, a little lower down to cover the wires of the first ring. Secure each ring with tape.

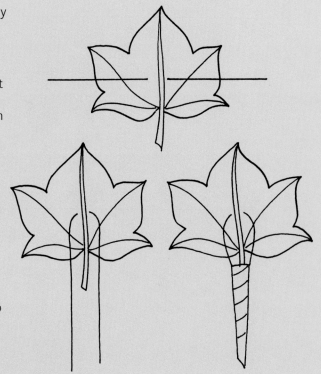

7 Cover the stems with ribbon to create a handle. Starting just below the leaves, wrap the ribbon round and round, rough side up (satin side against the stems), down the length of the stems so that each wrap overlaps the previous by 50 per cent.

8 Once you have reached 12 cm (5 in) twist the ribbon so that the satin side is facing upward. Wind it back upwards to the centre. Cut, then fold, the end over so no frayed edges show. Secure with pearl-headed pins. Insert at a vertical slant so they do not pierce the other side of the handle.

above A mass of *Rosa* 'Vendela', with a *Galax* leaf outer surround, creates a simple but timeless wedding bouquet.

Tip

You could loop *Aspidistra* leaves (see page 212) and place these around the bouquet in place of the wired leaves.

Tied posy

In recent years, the tied posy has been a popular design for both bridesmaids and brides. It is a very pretty and encapsulates the notion of informally picked flowers from the meadow. Unless you have a cutting garden this can be a more expensive and time-consuming option than the massed rose bouquet. Do remember that delicate flowers such as sweet peas have a short life.

The rose offers a strong round form and the other plant material gives contrast of texture, interest and fragrance. This design would not work without the strength of the roses or a similar flower with a strong form that is in harmony with the rest of the plant material – you just need a few to give dominance. It is the careful choice of plant material with a view to colour, form and texture that will give you success. Putting the stems together is easy.

Mixed posy with herbs

Handtieds of mixed flowers and foliage have become very fashionable over the past few years. Fragrance is much loved by most brides and the introduction of herbs and sweet-smelling flowers into a bouquet is always appreciated.

You will need

- **roses – garden roses are ideal**
- **garden flowers of choice (optional)**
- **a mix of foliage that complement the form and texture of the roses such as grey *Senecio cineraria*, lavender, mint, myrtle, spray roses, rosemary or other herbs**
- **garden twine**
- **1 m (3 ft 3 in) satin or wire-edged ribbon about 2.5 cm (1 in) wide**
- **pearl-headed pins.**

Method

1 Remove most of the leaves from the stems, leaving a few at the top. Place the stems in the left hand (if you are right-handed) and add the flowers with the right hand. Keep the stems straight but make a gentle dome of flowers. Trim the stems fairly short, usually no more than 20 cm (8 in). Leave the stems exposed.

2 Wrap with a wide satin ribbon as described in step 7 of the handtied wedding bouquet on page 271. Alternatively use raffia and secure with pearl-headed pins.

Tip

If the design is made in advance of the occasion (which is advisable), leave the posy overnight in a cool place, in an appropriate-size vase that will not damage the flowers. Spray gently with water.

left A mixed bouquet of *Freesia*, *Hydrangea* florets, *Hypericum* berries and roses.

right Beautiful, fragrant garden roses are mixed with *Alchemilla mollis* and lavender foliage to give a fragrant summer bouquet.

Buttonholes and corsages

Buttonholes are traditionally worn by the groom and best man. They are simple and traditionally made with one flower and a few leaves. Today extra embellishments are often added. They originate from medieval times, when a knight would wear his lady's colours as a declaration of love, and today the grooms' buttonhole often uses a flower seen the bride's bouquet. They are pinned to the left lapel.

Corsages, traditionally worn by the ladies in the wedding party, are more difficult to create and require a comprehensive knowledge of wiring. Consequently they are best left to the florist in charge. They are worn on the right.

below Today, an elaborate buttonhole and a simple corsage are often one and the same. This wired design of a single rose, smooth-textured leaf, *Hypericum* berries and *Senecio cineraria* leaves – finished with loops of flexi grass – create an elegant piece for the dress or suit lapel.

left A single rose with a surround of two leaves is a typical buttonhole for the men in the bridal party.

Rose and ivy buttonhole

This classic rose design is easy to make if you follow these step by step instructions. Wired work is always best made the day of the occasion. However if time is at a premium your buttonhole can be wrapped in damp tissue paper, placed in a plastic bag and kept in the vegetable compartment of the fridge over night.

You will need

to wire the rose
- 1 medium-size rose
- 0.71 mm wire
- 0.56 mm wire (if it is difficult to find different gauges of wire use two 0.71 wires)

to wire the leaves
- 2–3 green, small to medium-size ivy leaves
- 2–3 florists' wires – 0.28 mm or 0.32 mm

Plus
- stem tape
- pin

Method

1 Cut the rose short, leaving about 2.5 cm (1 in) of stem. Place an internal support wire through the short stem, using a 0.71 mm wire. Take this as far as the seed box. Be careful not to pierce the petals as they will bruise.

2 Take a lighter- or similar-gauge wire and take it through the seed box horizontally, in one side and out the other. Bring the two equal lengths of wire down to lie parallel with the first wire. There is no need to wrap any of the wires together.

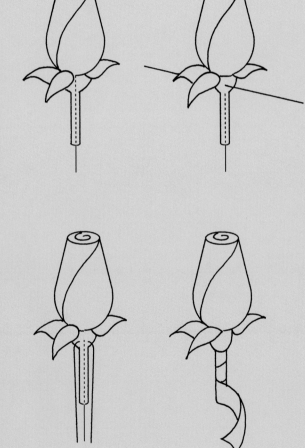

3 Take the stem tape and cover the stem and wire. Be sure to cover the point where the wire meets the stem. It is not necessary to cover too much of the stem, since it will be cut shorter. The tape needs to be stretched so finely it nearly snaps. If you are right-handed twirl the wire with your left hand and with your right pull the tape taut away and down at approximately a 130-degree angle. If left-handed perform this action in reverse.

4 Next you need to wire a leaf. Follow the instructions on page 270 – step 4.

5 As an option, wire other flowers, berries or leaves to be included. However, a buttonhole is usually quite simple.

6 Arrange the rose and leaves together so that the leaves frame but do not obscure the flower.

7 Take the stem tape and wrap tightly round the wire stems to form one single stem. Ensure the end is sealed completely and that no bare wires are showing, Cut to an appropriate length.

ACKNOWLEDGEMENTS

Special thanks

Writing a book is a long, complex process – and it is only by working with inspirational professionals that it succeeds.

With *Flower Arranging, The Complete Guide*, I have been aided and abetted by a team of wonderful people. My thanks go to Georgina Goldsmith, Tomasz Koson and Tomoko Godfrey at the Flower School, who helped with photography and design, Lesley Levene and Emma Dawson for their excellent proof reading, Laura Leong and Rachel Poole for the artwork, my teachers at the school, former students, members of NAFAS and so many more.

The photographers – in particular Clive, Oliver, Toby and Tom – have made the photoshoots most enjoyable and fun experiences and have created excellent images with an eye for perfect detail.

Dr Christina Curtis is a good friend and colleague who has a knowledge of botanical nomenclature second to none. She has ensured that the plant names are correct and match the photographs – not an easy task!

I would also like to thank Barry, Brian, Dave, Russell and Tom at Porters Foliage and Bobby and Dennis at Alagar, New Covent Garden Market for their invaluable advice. Also thanks to Jenny and Hans at Metz and Ian and Angelica at Flowervision for their input on purchasing flowers. Rococo Chocolates provided their sumptuous eggs for the design on page 195. A big thank you to Malcolm at Two Peas in a Pod in Barnes for his wonderful rhubarb and leeks. As always the best in town!

Tom and Nikki Edwards had the most marvellous wedding at Burghley House and they have kindly allowed me to use Darren Cresswell's images. Flowers at Chicheley Hall was a fantastic event with superb designers from all over the world – my grateful thanks to those whose work appears in this book.

My thanks and appreciation to the ever patient, ever tolerant family – David, Charles, Jane and my mother Joan, who at the youthful age of 91 helped proof read this book.

Lastly my heart-felt gratitude to Amanda Hawkes, a designer par excellence whose dedication to perfection is combined with a rare gift for design and true professionalism.

Floral designers

All the designs in this book are by Judith Blacklock except for those listed below. Many thanks to these designers for allowing The Flower Press to reproduce their work:

page 47, 137, 219: Felix Geiling-Rasmus
page 57, 249, 261, 267 (top), 272: Dawn Jennings
page 65: Mo Duffill
page 73: Jean Pierre Bonello
page 77 (top), 109, 154, 245: Georgina Goldsmith
page 81: Ann-Marie Kendrick
page 90: Laura Bates
page 91, 10, 131, 132, 135, 136, 145, 235: Tomasz Koson
page 96–97, 206, 209 (left): Stef Adrienssens
page 107: Home Counties Area of NAFAS
page 110, 173, 201, 211: Unknown
page 112, 220: Robert Koene
page 120: Annette Parshotam
page 133: Wendy Andrade
page 167, 169, 171, 244: Ann-Marie Kendrick and
    Judith Blacklock
page 150: South Midlands Area of NAFAS
page 166, 199: Inspired by Alison Penno
page 168, 236–237, 259: The Flower School team
page 175, 198: Lynne Dallas
page 177: Judith Blacklock and Ashleigh Hopkins
page 179: Susan Philips
page 186: Jenny Bennett
page 195: Delrose Earle
page 205: Inspired by Judith Taylor
page 217: Stijn Simaeys
page 218, 222–3: Laura Leong
page 240 (bottom), 256–257: Robbie Honey
page 241, 267 (bottom): Tanya Ferguson
page 240 (top), 262–263: Miss Pickering
page 251: David Thomson
page 252: Emberton Flower Club
page 260: Neil Bain
page 262–263: Miss Pickering
page 264: Amanda Hawkes

PHOTOGRAPHIC CREDITS

Photographers

Judith Blacklock: 7, 9, 43 (bottom), 57, 67, 70 (bottom), 73, 74, 75, 76, 78, 79, 91, 101, 108, 109, 110, 111, 136, 137, 144 (top), 144 (bottom), 146, 147, 148 (top), 148 (bottom), 151, 156, 157, 158, 161, 162–3, 164–5, 166–7 (bottom), 168–169 (bottom), 175, 179, 181, 191, 192, 193, 209, 210, 228, 229, 232, 236, 240 (top), 249, 251, 255, 259, 262 (top), 265, 267 (top), 271, 273

Darren Cresswell (www.darrencresswellphotography.co.uk): 149, 166–167 (top), 170–171, 244, 262 (bottom), 263

Thomas de Hoghton (www.tdehphotography.co.uk): 60–61, 124–25, 126–27, 133, 135, 145, 152, 153, 177, 184, 190, 194, 225, 234, 235, 246, 248, 260, 274

Tanya Ferguson (www.floral-accents.co.uk): 241, 267

Oliver Gordon (www.olivergordon.co.uk): Front cover, 1, 3, 4, 48, 49, 51, 55, 63, 68–69, 80, 81, 83, 85, 93, 99, 100, 102, 104, 105, 106, 107, 112, 113, 114 (bottom), 115, 116, 117, 118, 119, 120, 122, 129, 131, 132, 139, 141, 142, 150, 182, 186, 188, 196 (bottom), 198, 202, 211, 217, 218, 220, 223, 224, 226-227, 237, 238–239, 245, 247, 252–3, 261, 266, 268, 269, 272, 275

Alice Hall (www.alicehall.eu): 50, 209 (right)

David Hawkes: 45, 264

D.W.F. Hallett (www.countyflorist.co.uk): 6 (top),43

Chrissie Harten (www.thegardener.btinternet.co.uk): 42 (top), 47, 65, 70 (top), 71, 90, 96–97, 114 (top), 201, 206, 207, 219

Robbie Honey (www.robbiehoney.com): 155, 240 (bottom), 257–258

International Flower Bulb Bureau: 88, 103, 121, 123, 203

Ash Mills (www.ashmills.com): 243

Clive Nichols (www.clivenichols.com): 58, 59, 200, 230–231

Toby Smith (www.shootunit.com): 86, 197, 216, 166–167 (bottom), 197, 208, 215, 216, 233

Courtesy of *The Flower Arranger*: 186

Photo credits

The publishers wish to thank the following photographers and organisations for permission to reproduce their photographs:

page 6 (bottom): © fotolinchen/iStockphoto.com
page 15 (top right): © Hgalina – Fotolia.com
page 15 (bottom right): © Svenja98 – Fotolia.com
page 16 (bottom left): © Vital Paplauski/iStockphoto.com
page 20 (top centre): © Ashley Whitworth – Fotolia.com
page 20 (top right): © Tamara Kulikova – Fotolia.com
page 20 (bottom left): © Profotokris – Fotolia.com
page 23 (top left): © masterzphotofo – Fotolia.com
page 23 (top centre): © Elena Schweitzer – Fotolia.com
page 23 (bottom left): © Yuris – Fotolia.com
page 23 (bottom centre): © nataliavand – Fotolia.com
page 24 (top right): © Volker Z – Fotolia.com
page 24 (bottom centre): © thongsee – Fotolia.com
page 25 (bottom right): © rawlik – Fotolia.com
page 38 (top right): © Hgalina – Fotolia.com
page 87 (bottom right): © brytta/iStockphoto.com
page 113 (top left): © Elena Schweitzer – Fotolia.com
page 113 (top right/sunflower): © Ruslan Semichev – Fotolia.com
page 113 (top right/craspedia): Craig Holdway – Fotolia.com
page 173: © Richard Viard/iStockphoto.com
page 178 (gladiolus): © Karol Zieliński – Fotolia.com
page 178 (hydrangea): © Tamara Kulikova – Fotolia.com
page 178 (alstroemeria): © Nadezda Verbenko – Fotolia.com

OTHER TITLES FROM
THE FLOWER PRESS

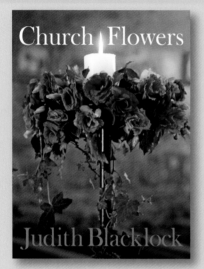